RESEARCH LIBRARY
OF
COLONIAL AMERICANA

INCREASE MATHER
VS.
SOLOMON STODDARD

Two Puritan Tracts

ARNO PRESS
A New York Times Company
New York – 1972

Reprint Edition 1972 by Arno Press Inc.

The Order of the Gospel...was reprinted from
a microfilm copy furnished by the University
of Illinois Library.
The Doctrine of Instituted Churches Explained...
was reprinted from a microfilm copy furnished
by The Union Theological Seminary Library.

LC# ·72-141117
ISBN 0-405-03328-1

Research Library of Colonial Americana
ISBN for complete set: 0-405-03270-6
See last pages of this volume for titles.

Manufactured in the United States of America

Publisher's Note: The selections in this
compilation were reprinted from the best
available copies.

CONTENTS

The Order of the

Gospel,

Professed and Practised by the Churches of CHRIST in *New England*, Justified, by the Scripture, and by the Writings of many Learned men, both Ancient and Modern Divines ; In Answer to several Questions, relating to Church Discipline

By *Increase Mather*, President of *Harvard Colledge* in *Cambridge*, and Teacher of a Church at *Boston* in *New England*.

Jer. 2. 21, 36 *I had planted thee a noble vine, wholly a right seed ···· why gaddest thou about so much to change thy way ?···*
Col 2. 5 *Joying and beholding your Order, ··· and the Steadfastness of your Faith.*

BOSTON, Printed by B. Green, & J. Allen, for Nicholas Buttolph, at his Shop at the Corner of Gutteridges Office House. 1700.

The Epistle Dedicatory.

TO THE
Churches of CHRIST
IN
New-England.

THA'T the Churches which are called *Reformed*, have attained unto but an *Imperfect Reformation*, is a Truth not to be denyed : The defect has not been so much in *Doctrine* as in *Worship and Discipline*. Nevertheless, in this respect some Churches have gone beyond others. In *Geneva, France, Holland*, they have made an higher Progress then in *Germany* : of which the chief *Reformers*, such as *Melancthon, Martyr, Musculus, Zanchy* and others were very sensible, bitterly complaining that many who were willing to cast off *the yoke of Antichrist,*

3   A 2   yet

yet were not willing to Subject to *the Yoke of Christ*. Amongst all the Reformed Churches, some have given the Preference to the *Bohemian-Brethren*, who sprang from the *Waldenses*, and they from the true Apostolick Church, not corrupted with Popery. These did *Luther* in the year 1524. mislike, because of their *strict Ecclesiastical Discipline*. But twelve years after that, he saw cause to alter his Judgement, and write in Defence of those Holy Churches, which once he had written against, bewayling his own Error in that he had been so Lax in Admissions to the Lords Table, and wishing that the *Evangelics* in *Germany*, had began *the Reformation* with *Discipline*, and not with *Doctrine* only. For which change of his Judgement Popish Authors do unworthily upbraid him, since it was a change for the better. *Lasitius* (the Polish Historian) sayes, that if any where in the World *the Primitive Apostolical Churches* were to be seen, it was amongst the *Ecclesiolæ*, the poor little Churches of the *Bohemian Brethren*. When Learned *Bucer* heard one of their Ministers (who was sent on purpose into *Germany* for that end) give an account of *the Order of their Churches*, he burst out into Tears, saying to the other Divines Present, *This is Heaven upon Earth*. *Vergerius*, (that famous Preacher who having been the *Popes Legat* to the Emperor, taking *Calvins Institutions* into his hands with a design to confute him, was Converted thereby) wrote to an

Eminent

Eminent Person in those Churches, that he Prayed for nothing in this world so much as that he might Live and Dye a member amongst them. Now that wherein these Churches did chiefly Excel, was their *Order* Especially in *their great strictness as to Admissions to the Lords Supper.* It was in those dayes objected against them, *Fratres non habent Ecclesiam apertam,* that their *Churches were enclosures,* and their Church doors were too strait. But they knew that the Scripture calls the Church a *Garden Enclosed, a Spring shut up, and a fountain Sealed. Cant.* 4. 12. They were wont to Answer such as made that objection against them, *Christ has taught us that we must not give Holy things, Except to Holy Persons. Religion* (said they) *is not to begin with the Sacrament, but with Repentance and Faith. And as Christ would not commit himself to all that Professed Faith, so neither must we. There are many that prove* Abortive Christians, *we must be as careful as we can, that we be not deceived with such Communicants. And therefore the Consciences of such as offer themselves to our Communion are to be searched into, and they must be tryed concerning their sincerity again and again ; and Observation made what Fruits that are Evidences of true Repentance do appear in them.* This was the Doctrine : This was the Discipline of those famous Churches. Thus did they Practise for many years. But by reason of an *Universal Toleration,* and through *Corruption in their Schools,* they degenerated, and wonderfully loft their Difcipline, until the Jealoufy of the Lord diffipated and deftroyed them all. A late writer ob-ferves, that for the fpace of *Forty years* the *Reformed* Churches in *France* kept clofe to their *Ecclefiaftical Difcipline,* but after that they grew remifs. And what has God done to them all at this day? It was fpoken to the Church in *Ephefus,* Rev. 2. 4, 5. *Thou haft left thy firft Love, Remember therefore whence thou art fallen, and do the firft works, or elfe I will come to thee quickly, and will remove thy Candleftick out of his place.* The *Revelation* was written *Forty years* after the Church in *Ephefus* was firft planted. The *Firft Generation* of Church Members in that time were doubtlefs the moft of them dead : their Succeffors wanted *the Firft Zeal* for the wayes of Chrift wherein their Predeceffors had Excelled. This at laft iffued in a Removal of the Candleftick.

And fhould not the dear Churches of *New-England,* be awakened by fuch awful Examples to take heed laft it be thus with them? And therefore to beware of *Declenfions,* either from *the Fiath* or from *the Order* of the Gofpel. There is that which the Scripture call, *the prefent Truth,* in which in a fpecial manner we ought to be *Eftablifhed.* 2 Pet. 1. 12. *viz.* That which is very Peculiarly the Truth of the Age or the Place where the Divine Providence has caft our Lot. And this is *Now* the Truth which doa concern *Ecclefiaftical Polity.*

The Epistle Dedicatory. 7

Polity. That is it, for which our Fathers suffered a *Voluntary Exile* into this Wilderness, when it was a Land not Sown. Here God rewarded them with shewing to them *the form of his House, with all the outgoings thereof, and all the comings in thereof.* Mr *Brightman,* before ever there was a *New England,* Conjectured that there would be some Faithful Servants of Christ in a *Wilderness,* unto whom he should make *Singular Discoveries* of Truth ; which several Judicious Authors have Esteemed as a Prophetical Passage fulfilled in what has come to pass in this *American Desert.* However, The Truths which respect *Church Order* are they which these Churches above any other are concerned to maintain : And an *Apostacy* from them would in *New-England* be a greater Sin and Provocation to Christ, then in any Place in the whole world. *Regenvolscius* in his *Ecclesiastical History* of the *Sclavonian Churches,* relates that *Lucas Brugensis,* (a man famous for his Learning and Piety amongst the *Bohemians,*) was wont to say, that he did not so much dread all the Enemies and Persecutors whom they were continually endangered by, as he was *afraid least remissness in their Holy Discipline would prove the ruin of their Churches.* His *Prediction* was sadly verified. I pray God the like fate may never attend these Churches, in too many of which there is an amazing *Relaxation of Discipline.* Sure I am, that *to depart from the Order of the Gospel* established in these Churches in the

the dayes of our Fathers, and declared in *the Platform of Discipline,* is not the way to obtain such signal Divine protections as they were favoured with. *Isa.* 4. 5　If we Espouse such principles as these, Namely, *That Churches are not to Enquire into the Regeneration of those whom they admit unto their Communion. That Admission to Sacraments is to be left wholly to the prudence and Conscience of the Minister. That Explicit Covenanting with God and with the Church is needless. That Persons not Qualified for Communion in special Ordinances shall Elect Pastors of Churches. That all Professed Christians have right to Baptism. That Brethren are to have no Voice in Ecclesiastical Councils. That the Essence of a Ministers call is not in the Election of the People, but in the Ceremony of Imposing hands. That Persons may be Established in the Pastoral Office without the Approbation of Neighbouring Churches or Elders ;* We then give away *the whole Congregational cause* at once, and a great part of the *Presbyterian Discipline* also. To begin a change in one of these Particulars without *Decision of a Synod,* would in other Churches of the *Reformed* be counted *Presumption* ; but to design all or most of these *Innovations* at once, is certainly a *bold Attempt*　No longer since then *May* 27 1697. no less then Thirty Ministers in this *Province,* did declare and subscribe it with their hands, *That they were made sensible of the tendencies which there are amongst us towards Deviations from*

from the good *Order* wherein our *Churches* have according to the *Word* of the *Lord Jesus Christ*, been happily *established* and continued There is cause to be sensible of it now as much as then. For *Deviations* are not less then formerly, but rather growing upon us every day. Shall we then by silence betray the Truth ? When the interest of *Christ* is concerned ; do we not hear that voice, *Who is on the Lords Side* ? *Who* ? Is there no one that will stand up for the Churches of *Christ* ? The Good People in them may then well think that their *Watchmen* are all either Dead or Asleep : For which cause it is, that I *Dedicate* this ensuing *Dissertation* unto you *the Churches of Christ* in *New-England.*

My Brethren, and the Lords People.

It is not *my own Cause*, but *Yours*, which I have here undertaken and plead for. Did I say *Yours* ? Nay, it is *Christs Cause.* The defence of these Truths is now become *the Cause of Christ and of his Churches in New-England.* I am also very sensible that *Young Divines*, who have not Studied these *Controversies*, are apt to think, that what has been *Ordinarily professed and practised in the Churches of New England,* is *Novelty* and *Singularity.* It may in that respect be a Service to the Churches that something be written, which may be for the Information and Illumination of such, in *Questions* of this nature,

by

by means whereof they may be the more fit to Serve the *Churches of God* wherever the Divine Providence shall see good to dispose of them.

New-England (I mean the Churches in it) was *Planted a Noble Vine wholly a righ seed.* We are all concerned in our several Capacities (Ministers in theirs and People in theirs) to Labour what in us lies, that they who shall come after us, may not prove *Degenerate Plants* ; much more should we Endeavour that they may not be so in our Dayes. It is a sad Observation often Verified by Experience, That *Religion in the Purity and Power of it, seldome continues long in the same place.* When the *Church of Israel* was in a Setled State, *They Served the Lord all the dayes of Joshua, and of the Elders that out lived Joshua ; that Generation was gathered to their Fathers, and there arose another Generation after them which knew not the Lord. They turned quickly out of the way which their Fathers walked in, obeying the Voice of the Lord, but they did not so.* It was the *third Generation* of Church Members which proved Degenerate and Apostate : Pray God it be not so in *New-England.* The *First Generation* of his Servants whom he brought into this Wilderness are gathered to their Fathers : And many of the *Second Generation,* such of them as are yet living are now in years, and soon will be all gone. The *Third Generation* are coming to take their turn.

Some

Some of them are great Blessings to the Churches, as inheriting the Principles, Spirit, and Grace of their Fathers and Grand-Fathers, but many of them do not so. On which account, it is not at all to be wondred at, if they Dislike *the Good Old way of the Churches;* yea, if they Scoff at it, as some of them do; or if they are willing *to depart from what is Ordinarily Practised in the Churches of Christ in New-England.* For *the Congregational Church Discipline,* is not Suited for a Worldly Interest, or for a *Formal Generation* of Professors. It will stand or fall as *Godliness in the Power of it* does prevail or otherwise. That there is a great decay of the Power of Religion throughout all *New England* is Lamentably true. If that revive, there will be no fear of *Departing* from the Holy Discipline of the Churches of Christ. But revived it will be amongst those who are Enemies to *Explicit Covenanting* with God and His People, against whom the *Religious Societies of the Church of England Communion,* now in *London,* will rise up and Condemn them. Was it ever known that *Collapsed Churches* were restored to their Primitive State of Purity, but in this way, and by this means of *Explicit Renovation* of their Covenants with God and with one another. But I hope enough is said about that in the Subsequent *Disquisition.*

Let the Churches Pray for the *Colledge* particularly, that God may ever Bless that Society with faithful *Tutors* that will be true to Christs

Interest

Interest and theirs, and not Hanker after new and loose wayes. This is a matter of no small concernment. For if the Fountain whose *Streams should make glad the City of God,* be corrupted, Posterity will be Endangered thereby. The poor Churches in *Bohemia* before mentioned found it so. If the begun *Apostacy* should proceed as fast the next thirty years as it has done these last, surely it will come to that in *New-England* (Except the Gospel it self *Depart* with the *Order* of it) that the most Conscientious People therein, will think themselves concerned to gather Churches out of Churches. But as yet the *Declension* is not gone so far but a Stop may be put thereunto, and the Interest of Religion be Retrieved. It was said to one of he decaying Churches in *Asia, Be watchful and strengthen the things which remain, and are ready to Dy; ... Remember how thou hast received, and heard, and hold fast.* Do's not the Lord Jesus Christ say so to the Churches in *New-England:*) And does He not say, as unto another of the Churches, *Hold fast that thou hast, that no man take thy Crown.*

The Lord give us Grace so to do, which is the hearts desire and Prayer, of him who is,

Yours to Serve you,

Increase Mather

B*ston.* 1*m.*
1700.

THE
Order of the Churches
in New-England.
VINDICATED.

QUESTION I.

*W*Hether *Particular Churches ought to Consist of Saints and true Believers on Christ?*

The Question is not *de facto*, whether there are not true Churches in whom there are many that are not Saints, but *de jure*, whether it ought to be so? and whether that Church is not Guilty of Sin, which dos admit those into their Communion who are not in the Judgment of rational Charity, true Believers on Christ. This being premised for the true stating of the *Question*; the Answer is *Affirmative.* And that for these amongst other Reasons.

B   1. The

1. There are Scripture predictions relating to the Times of the New-Testament which intimate that *Evangelical Churches* shall consist of *Holy Persons*. It is foretold that the uncircumcised shall not Enter into Gods Holy City. *Isai.* 52. 1. That *the high way*, the way into the Church should be *the way of Holiness. Isai.* 35. 8. That the people should be *all Righteous, the branch of the Lords planting, the work of his hands that He might be glorifyed Isai* 60. 21. That unsanctified persons shall be kept out of the Spiritual Jerusalem, *Rev.* 21. 27.

2. The Scripture informs us that in Churches where the appointment of Christ was observed it has been thus. As in *Ephesus, Corinth, Philippi, Colosse,* the members of the Churches there, were *Saints, Faithful Brethren, Sanctified in Christ Jesus.*

3. A particular instituted Church is the House of God. That particular Church in *Ephesus* is said to be so. 1 *Tim* 3. 15. A (*a*) Learned and Eminent Divine has these Expressions. As (saith he) a vertuous Civil man ' dos not like to have in his House uncivil ' persons, so the most Holy God will not ' allow any to be in his Family, that are ' unholy. As no man can think well to have ' Swine in his House, or Dogs and Swine to ' come to board with the rest of the Family, ' so open Sinners have no allowance from God ' to be in his Household.

4. None

(*a*) *Mr. Paul Bain on Eph.* 1. *p.* 91. 111.

4. None that were legally unclean might enter into the Jewish Temple, 2 *Chron.* 23. 19. *Act.* 21. 28, 29. Nor Eat of the Paſover and other Holy things. *Numb.* 9 6, 10, 11. Now Evang'lical Churches are the Lords Temple. 1 *Cor* 3. 16, 17. And 2 *Cor.* 6. 16. And they have in them Sacred things, yea the Body and Blood of Chriſt; and therefore they who are Morally Unclean may not be admitted into them. The Ceremonial Holineſs of the Jewiſh Church was *Typical* of that real Holineſs which ought to be in Goſpel Churches.

5. When it has been otherwiſe, the Lord has reproved them that have cauſed or permitted ſuch abuſes; as in the Church at *Corinth, Pergamus, Thyatira,* which are blamed for their ſuffering Ungodly perſons to be in their Communion 1 *Cor.* 5 2, 13. *Rev.* 2. 14, 15, 20 A Scripture which has reſpect unto the Times of the Goſpel ſeverly rebukes thoſe Miniſters which ſhall bring men that are *Uncurcumciſed in Heart,* (Unregenerate perſons) *into the Sanctuary,* into the Church of God, *to Eat the Bread and Drink the Blood* which they that are there partake of, *Ezek:* 44, 7, 9

6 Nothing can be more fatal to the Intereſt of Religion, then to Conſtitute Churches of Unſanctified Members This made way for the *Antichriſtian Apoſtacy,* which has been Subverſive to the Intereſt of Chriſt and Holineſs throughout the greateſt part of that which bears the Name of *Chriſtendome.* When

B 2 Chriſtianity

Christianity became the State Religion, whole Provinces at once were made Church-Members, upon a bare Profession of Christianity, without any regard to their real Sanctity. And this Corrupting the Church as to the matter of it, was the means of introducing that Corruption in Doctrine, Worship, Order, which soon followed. Of this some of the *Ancients* who lived in *the fourth Century* were very sensible, for we find in their Writings sad complaints about it. If we allow a Degeneracy in our Churches in respect of the matter of them our *Dethels* will soon become *Bethavens*. It is a smart but a true Expression of a Great (b) Divine, *That to compose Churches of habitual Sinners, and that either as to Sins of Commission or Sins of Omission, is not to Erect Temples to Christ, but Chappels to the Devil.*

Nor is this Assertion, *That Visible Saints are the matter of a particular Church* a notion peculiar unto *Congregational Men.* Our Brethren of the *Presbyterian Parswasion* say the same thing. Yea, *the good old Non-conformists,* and all that have been Studious of *Reformation* in the Church concur in this principle. Mr. *Ball* (c) who was of the Presbyterian Judgment, sayes, *That all true Churches should consist of Visible Saints. The Non-conformists do acknow-*
ledge

(b) Dr. *Owen of a Gospel Church.*
part 2. p. 4.
(c) *Answer to Cann. part 2. p. 49. 50.*

ledge that *Churches planted and gathered accor-ding to Gods Word consists of Saints only.* Thus Mr. *Bal.* The Presbyterians of the Union in *London* have it for one of their Articles, *That none shall be Admitted as Members in order to Communion in all the special Ordinances of the Gospel, but such persons as are Knowing & Sound in the Fundamental Doctrines of the Christian Religion, without Scandal in their Lives, and to a Judgment regulated by the word of God, are persons of Visible Godliness and Honesty, credibly professing cordial Subjection to Jesus Christ.* Worthy Mr. *Rutherford* has these words, (†) *Those only* (sayes he) *are to be admitted to the Supper of the Lord, whom in Charity, we Judge, can and do Try and Examine themselves, and rightly discern the Lords Body, and who in Faith can annuatiate the Lords Death* The Churches in *New-England* are free to admit those into their Communion who are thus qualified: Nor do they insist on more.

(†) *Plea for the Presbytery in* Scotland. *p.* 184.

QUESTION. II.

WHether there ought not to be a Tryal of persons concerning their *Qualifications* and *Fitness for Church Communion* before they are *Admitted thereunto* ?

The Answer may be given in three Assertions.

B 3 1. WE

1. We Affirm that Examination and Tryal of the persons who offer themselves to our Sacred Communion whether they are duely qualified for it, is ordinarily neceffary.

For,

1. If men profeffing and pretending to be Apoftles were to be tryed whether they were fo indeed or no, then there is the like reafon that men pretending to be Saints, and fo fit materials for Church Fellowfhip, fhould be tryed whether they be fo or no. But the former is plain from *Rev* 2. 2. Where fuch perfons were tryed and found to be but Counterfeits.

2. In the Old Teftament there were perfons fet at the Gates of the Temple to fee who they were that did Effay to enter, and to keep thofe out that were not duely qualified. 2 *Chron.* 23. 19. And fhall the New Teftament Temple, *i. e.* the Church of God, have no perfons to Examine fuch as would enter thereinto? If Ceremonial uncleannefs made men unfit to enter into the Material Temple, Moral Uncleannefs renders them uncapable of Admiffion into the Spiritual Temple. Wherefore an Examination is neceffary.

3. It is faid of the *Myftical Jerufalem,* that Twelve Angels were at her Gates, *Rev.* 21. 12. Which does not obfcurely intimate, that there are Officers in the Chriftian Churches whofe work it is to obferve who they are that Effay to enter thereinto, that fo the

worthy

worthy or duely qualified may be admitted and others be debarred. from Enterance.

2. The tryal to be used should be such as may make it appear to the Judgement of rational Charity, that the persons be so qualified as all Church Members ought to be. It has been proved that *Church Members* ought to be *Believers*, *Saints*, *Regenerate* persons, And therefore the Church should put the persons who desire Admission into their Holy Communion, to declare and show whether it be thus with them, whether they have truly Repented of their Sins, and whether they truly Believe on Christ. Thus we read that *Philip* Examined the Eunuch whether he did believe on Christ with all his Heart or no, *Act.* 8. 37, And *John Baptist* put those whom he admitted to his Baptism to manifest their unfeigned Repentance. *Matth.* 3. 2.

Nevertheless,

3. A rigid Severity in Examination is to be avoided, and such tenderness and Charity ought to be used as that the weakest Christians if Sincere may be encouraged and gladly admitted. Yea, it were better (as Mr. *Cotton* (d) observes) to admit diverse Hypocrites then to keep out one Sincere Child. of God from coming into the Church.

For,

1 Our Lord Jesus Christ would not break the bruised Reed nor quench the Smoaking flax. *Matth.* 12. 20. But gather the tender Lambs

C11

(d) *In the way of the Churches: p. 58.*

in his arms, and carry them gently in his bosome. *Isa* 40. 11.

2. Such as are weak in the Faith we are Expresly Commanded to receive. *Rom.* 14. 1. Receiving into Church fellowship may well (amongst other things) be comprehended in that Expression.

3. Weak Christians if Sincere have the Substance of that Faith and Sanctity which is necessarily required in Church Members ; and therefore no reason they should be Excluded, though. others may Exceed them in measure and degree of Knowledge and Grace.

4 Church Communion and the Ordinances of God belonging thereto, being of special use for Confirmation and growth in Grace, such Christians that are the weakest have the most need thereof, and therefore by no means should be Excluded there-from. These Rules being observed, we affirm that Examination of persons to be admitted into Communion at the Lords Table is necessary. More Arguments for it may be seen in Mr. *Cottons* Excellent Treatise of the *Holiness of Church Members.* And in this Controversy those of the *Presbyterian* perswasion agree with the *Congregational,* as we see in their *Vindication of the Presbyterial Government* published by the Ministers at *London* in the year 1650. Wherein what we assert is largly proved by many Reasons, and the usual Objections against it, are solidly answered. In the primitive Times they were very strict in Examining those
who

who were admitted into Church Fellowship.
The great *Chamier* wisheth that the like
strictness were used in these dayes. *Origen*
against *Celsus* (Lib. 3. p. Mihi. 142, 147,
148.) sayes, that in those dayes, *Christians*
did initiate none but Converted ones in their
Mysteries, and that they did all that possibly
they could do, that their Churches might consist
of none but such as were endued with Spiritual
Wisdom, and that therefore they that joyned to
them submitted to severe Examinations. This
principle, *That ungodly persons are not fit to*
be admitted to the Lords Table, was asserted in
the first dawnings of the *Reformation.* Not
only such as fell in with the *Geneva Discipline,*
but the *First Reformers* in the *Church of Eng-*
land went thus far. The Twenty nineth
Article sayes, *That in the use of the Lords Sup-*
per, such as are void of a Lively Faith, to their
Condemnation Eat and Drink the Sign and
Sacrament of the Body and Blood of Christ.
The *Liturgy* sayes, *That in no wise men should*
come but in the Marriage Garment. That if
any man be in Malice, or in any grievous Crime,
Let him not come to the Holy Table, but let
him Repent truely of his Sins past, and have
a lively Faith in our Saviour Christ. Such
Expressions as these are in the *English Liturgy.*
A. B *Cranmer* in his Answer to the Fifteenth
Articles of the Devonshire Rebels, having quoted
many old Canons which require the people
to Communicate and not the Priest alone,
has these words, *I would Exhort every Good*
Christian

Christian man often to receive the Holy Communion: yet I do not recite all these things to the intent that I would in this Corrupt World where men live so ungodly as they do, that the old Canons should be restored again, which Command every man present to receive the Communion with the Priest; which Canons if they were now used, I fear that men would receive it unworthily. See the *Appendix* to *Cranmers* Life lately published by Mr. *Strype* p 96. As for that objection that the *Sacrament* is a *Converting Ordinance*, and therefore that there is no need of Examining men about their Conversion in order to their being admitted to partake thereof, it is a Popish Assertion, Condemned and Confuted by our Divines, Excepting that some of the Grossest *Lutherans* have Espoused it. Diverse of our late Writers of the Presbyterian Judgment have Elaborately and Abundantly refuted that pernicious Error. Mr *Vines* calls this Opinion an *Upstart* Notion: And sayes, *He wonders that any should stand up in the defence of it since there is an army to a man against them.* See his Treatise of the Lords Supper. p. 215. Mr *Gillespy* in his *Aarons Rod Blossoming.* Book 3. 12, 13 and 14. Chapters, does not only Answer Mr *Prins* Allegations for the Affirmative, but he has by no less than Twenty Arguments with great Learning and Judgement demonstrated, that the Sacrament of the Supper is not a Converting but a Confirming Ordinance: otherwise it might be Administred

ministred not only to Ungodly but to Unbaptised persons.   An Ordinance appointed
for Conversion is not to be with-held from
Unbaptised persons: But the Lords Supper is
to be with held from Unbaptised persons.
Exod. 12. 48. Therefore &c.

QUESTION. III.

Whether are not the Brethren, and not the
Elders of the Church only to Judge concerning the Qualifications and Fitness of those
who are Admitted into their Communion?

Answ. There is some difference of Apprehension, and yet no breach of Amity or *Union*,
as to this *Question* between the Brethren of
the Presbyterian and the Congregational way,
the former giving this power only to the
Eldership, the later joyning the *Fraternity* with
them (e) Mr. *Cotton*, and from him Mr.
Norton has Judiciously stated and discussed
this Controversy.   Let their and some other
Arguments be duely weighed in the Ballance
of the Sanctuary.

1. They that have power in Admission
have power to Judge whether the persons to
be Admitted are duely qualified for Admission.
But this is true of the *Fraternity* as well as
of the *Presbytery*.   No one can be Admitted
into

(e) *In Resp. ad Apollon.* p. 13.

into the Church by the Elders without
the Consent of the Brethren. The Community is concerned in who are Admitted, and
therefore should concur therein. Its a received maxim, *Quod tangit omnes, debet ab omnibus approbari.* And reason sayes, They that
have power to Admit have power to Judge
whether the persons who desire it, are fit
for that Admittance.

2 They that have power to Judge whether a person is fit to be cast out of Communion, have power to Judge whether he is fit
to be received into Communion. *The Key*
{ the power } *of Opening and Shutting* belongs
to the same persons. But it is clear from
the Scripture, that the Brethren and not the
Elders only have power to Judge whether an
Offender is fit to be Excommunicated. *Matth.*
18. 17. *1 Cor.* 5. 12. All Orthodox Divine
agree that Church Discipline should be Exercised, *Consentiente plebe.* So amongst the
Ancients, *Cyprian, Ambrose, Austin, Jerom
Chrysostom, Nazianzene, Theodoret, Theophylact*
And amongst our Modren Divines, *Calvin
Beza, Bullinger, Melancton, Junius, Pareus
Rivet, Trelcatius.* If their consent is necessary
than they have power to Judge whether they
ought to consent or no.

3 They that have power to Judge whether
a person Excommunicated, is fit to be restored
to the Communion of the Church, have powe
to Judge whether persons never yet received
into the Communion of the Church are duely
qualifi.

qualified for that Communion.   But the A-
poſtle writes to *the Brethren* as well as to *the
Elders* of the Church in *Corinth* to reſtore a
penitent, whom they had according to the
diſcipline of Chriſt laid under a Church cenſure, *2 Cor. 2. 6.* If the Brethren are competent Judges cencerning the Repentance of a
Lapſed Communicant, they are not incom-
petent Judges of the Repentance of other perſons that may offer themſelves to their Communion.

4 When *Saul* deſired to joyn to the Church
at *Jeruſalem*, he was not admitted until the
Brethren were by the *Teſtimony* of *Barnabas,*
together with his own *Declaration,* ſatisfyed
concerning the reality of his Faith and Repentance. *Act 9 26, 27.*

5. If only Elders have power to Judge who
are fit to come to the Sacrament or to joyn
to the Churches, then in caſe there is but
one Elder in a Church (as there are very
few Churches in *New-England* that have more
Elders than one) the Sole power will reſide
in that one mans hands.   Then by a parity
of reaſon one alone would have power to
ſuſpend from Communion, which Judicious
Presbyterians do not allow of.   For the *London* Miniſters in their Vindication of the Presbyterian Government, (*p* 70,71.) have theſe
words. ' It is (ſay they) as warrantable by
' the word of God, for one Miniſter to aſſume
' unto himſelf alone the power of Suſpending
' from the Sacrament, as it is to aſſume the
        C   ' whole

' whole power of admitting to the Sacrament,
' for *contrariorum eadem est ratio*: For one
' Minister alone to assume this power to him-
' self, is to make himself a Congregational
' Pope. It is a bringing into the Church a
' power that would have some resemblance
' to Auricular Confession. Thus said the
Presbyterians Fifty years ago.

6. The way to keep Popery out of the
World, is for the *Fraternity* in Churches to
assert and maintain that power and priviledge, which does of right belong unto them.
Certain it is, that in the first Ages of Christianity this power which we plead for, was not
taken out of the hands of the Brother-hood.
One of the Ancients, whose writings give us
the greatest in-sight, into what was the general practice of the Churches, in the *Third
Century* makes this past dispute. In (f) one
of his Epistles he has these words, *Examina-
buntur Singela prusentibus et judicantibus vobis.*
And in another, *Vix plebi persuadeo at tales
patiantur admitti.* That he had much adoe
to perswade the people to be satisfied with
the Repentance and Qualifications of some
that desired a Reception or Restoration to
their Communion. When in after times
Church Members thought with themselves, our
Ministers understand Church Affairs better than
we do, therefore we will unconcern our selves,
and leave all to their *Conscience and Prudence*:
this very thing (as some Learned men have
observed) was that which made way for the

(f) *Cyprian. Epist* 40.   rise

rise of Popery. It may be it will be for the
Edification of some Readers, if we recite some
passages out of our famous Dr. *Owen*. In his
Judicious (g) Treatise of Evangelical Churches.
He has these words 'Dr. *Stillingfleet* denyes
' unto the people all Liberty or Ability to
' chuse their own Pastors, to judge what is
' meet for their own Edification, what is Heresy,
' or a pernicious Error, and what is not, or
' any thing of the like nature. This is al-
' most the same with that of the Pharisees,
' concerning them who admired and followed
' the Doctrine of our Saviour, *Joh.* 7. 49.
' *This people which know not the Law* : yet was
' it *this People*, whom the Apostle directed to
' choose out from among themselves persons
' meet for an Evangelical Office. *Act.* 6. *The*
' *same People* who joined with the Apostles
' and Elders in the consideration of the
' Grand case concerning the continuation of
' the Legal Ceremonies, and were Associates
' with them in the determination of it. *Act* 15.
' *The same* to whom all the Apostolical E-
' pistles, Excepting some to particular persons,
' were written.   And unto whom such di-
' rections were given and duties Enjoyned in
' them, as suppose not only Liberty and A-
' bility to judge for themselves in all matters
' of Faith and Obedience, but also an especial
' Interest in the Order and Discipline of the
' Church, those who were to say to *Archip-*
              C 2   ' *pus*

'pus their Bishop, *take heed to the Ministry*
'*which thou haft received in the Lord that thou*
'*fullfill it.* Col 4. 17. Unto whom of all forts
'it is Commanded that they should Examine
'and *Try Antichrifts, Spirits, and false Teachers,*
'that is, all forts of Hereticks, Herefies, and
'Errors. 1 *Joh. chap.* 2. 3. &c That people
'who even in following Ages adhered unto
'the Faith and the Orthodox profeffion of it,
'when almost all the Bishops were became
'Arian Hereticks. This principle of the Re-
'formation in Vindication of the Rights, Li-
'berties and Priviledges of the Christian Peo-
'ple to judge and choose for themselves in
'matters of Religion, to joyn freely in those
'Church Duties which are required of them,
'without which the work of it had never been
'carryed on, we do abide by and maintain.
'Yea, we meet with no Oppofition more
'fierce then upon the account of our afferting
'the Liberties and Rights of the People in
'reference unto Church Order and Worship
'But I shall not be afraid to say, that as the
'Reformation was begun and carryed on, on
'this principle : So when *this People* shall
'through an apprehenfion of their Ignorance,
'Weakness, and *Unmeetness to judge* in mat-
'ters of Religion, for themselves, and their own
'duty, be kept and debarred from it ; or
'when through their own floath, negligence,
'and vicioufness they shall be really unca·pa-
'ble to manage their own Interest in Church
'Affairs, as being fit only to be Governed

'if

' if not as *Bruit* Creatures, yet as *Mute* per-
' sons and that thefe things are improved by
' the Ambition of *the Clergy ingroffing all things*
' *in the Church to themfelves,* as they did in
' former Ages, if the *Old Popedome* do not
' return, a *New one* will be Erected as bad as
: the other.   Thus far Dr. *Owen.*

QUESTION. IV.

WHether is it neceſſary that perſons at their
Admiſſion into the Church, ſhould make
a publick Relation of the Time and Manner of
their Converſion ?

Anſw. 1   As the *Queſtion* is worded, the
Anſwer muſt be *Negative.*   Nor do the
Churches of *New England* impoſe this : nor
ought this to be required or deſired of every
one that joyns to our Communion:
          For,
   1. Some truly Converted ones know neither
the Time nor the Manner of their Converſion   It is often ſo with thoſe that have been
Advantaged with a Religious Education, and
that have been all their dayes kept from falling into Scandalous Sins.   The Spirit of God
changeth their Hearts gradually and inſenſibly,
as Mr. *Hooker* and other practical Divines
have ſhewen.   I have (*h*) elſe-where noted
          C 3   what

(*h*) *In the preface to Mr. Mitchels Life*

what Mr. *Baxter* relates concerning a confiderable number of Eminent Christians who being met together on other accounts, it was propofed whether they could all give an account of the Exact Time of their Converfion ; and there was but one of them all that could do it.

2. The natural Tempers and Infirmities of fome are fuch as make them uncapable of relating publickly what God has done for them. Some have a natural Hefitancy of Speech. Others are of very bafhful Tempers. Others are of fuch weak Intellectuals as that they can Scarce fpeak fence. To put fuch upon *Publick Declarations* of their Experiences, would be to expofe Sacred things to be Contemned and Ridiculed by men of profane Spirits.

3. It is poffible that the Occafion of a mans Converfion may have been fomething not fit to be publickly related. It may b the words of fome perfecuted Saint who is in obfcurity. It may be fome fignal Judgmen on fome of his Relations : Nay, it may b fome Secret Sin which himfelf has been guilty of, may have fo wounded his Confcience as to occafion his true Repentance for all hi other Sins : but this he ought not to tell the World of.

4. I am the more flow to pronounce th practice in Queftion to be *Abfolutely neceffary* for that, Good and wife men have not been

faireftyed

satisfyed neither with the necessity nor yet with the Expediency of it. True it is, that the reason of that Opposition against it which is in the minds of some, proceeds from their own want of Experience. The *American Apostle*, (as Mr. *Baxter* calls him) good old Mr. *Eliot*, who was very Zealous for publick Relations, has sometimes told us of a man that Joyned himself to the Church in *Roxbury*, who had been a very bitter Enemy to this Holy practice of the Churches in *New-England*, until the Lord changed his Heart : And then when he offered himself to the Communion of the Church, he began his publick Relation after this manner. *It may be it will be wondred at that I who have been such an Enemy to these Relations, and have so often inveighed against that practice of the Churches, should now be willing my self to Relate what impressions the Word and Spirit of God has made upon me. I must Confess, that when I was against that Practice, the true reason was because I had nothing to say ; but it has pleased the Lord to Open my eyes, and to Change my heart : and now I am willing to Declare unto all you that fear the Lord, what God has done for my Soul.* After this manner did that Converted man Express himself. Yet nevertheless, some who have had Experience of the Regenerating Grace of God in their own Souls, have not thought it necessary, to declare this Publickly, when they Joyn in Church-fellowship. I remember my Worthy Friend and

and Ancient acquaintance, the Reverend and Learned Mr. *John How* (who was Pastor of a Congregational Church in great *Torrington* in *Devonshire*, where I was his Successor in the work of the Ministry forty years agoe) informed me of one in that Church, who had been very averse to make a Relation of his Experiences, as supposing there was no Rule in Scripture obliging all that joyned to the Church so to practice : But at last he yielded to the Importunity of them that desired it from him ; and made such a Relation of the work of God on his Soul, that (as Mr *How* assured me) there was not one man in all the Church that had dry Eyes at the hearing of it. These things considered, we shall readily concede unto those who are Scrupulous about Relations, that *A Formal Relation is not absolutely necessary* in order to Admission into Church Fellowship.

Nevertheless,

Answ. 2. The practice of the Churches in *New England* as to this particular, is Lawful, Laudable, and Edifying. It is Lawful for Churches to desire those that offer themselves to their Holy Fellowship, to give an account of their Faith and Repentance : And when a Church desires it, no capable person ought to refuse it. For,

1 There is Scripture warrant for this practice. *David* sayes, *I have not hid thy Righteousness within my heart, I have declared thy Faithfulness and thy Salvation, I have not concealed thy*

loving

loving kindness and thy Truth from the great Congregation. Psal. 40. 10 And in another place, he sayes; *Come and hear all you that fear God, and I will declare what he has done for my Soul. Psal* 66 16. These Expressions show that a Christian should be willing upon just occasion, to declare the Goodness and Gracious workings of God upon his Soul, and this too in the Assembly and Congregation of his People Now if a Church does desire it, thats a just occasion for the doing of it : and therefore it then ought to be done. Moreover, the Scripture sayes, that Christians should be *ready to give a reason of the hope that is in them to every one that asketh.* I *Pet* 3. 15. This Expression of *A reason of their hope* shews that they must not only declare what good things they hoped for in this or in another world, but also upon what grounds they did so hope. For else they might shew their hope, but not *the Reason* of their hope. Now if a man has Experienced a work of Saving Conversion, causing him to accept of Christ on the terms of the Gospel, he has sufficient Ground and *Reason* for Hope. *Eph.* 1. 18. *Heb.* 11. 1. But without that he has no reason to hope but the contrary. *Eph.* 2. 12. Therefore he that declares the reason of his hope, must declare his Faith and Regeneration. If the Apostle does specially intend that Christians should be ready to do this before Persecutors, who would probably be offended with them for

it,

it, surely they should be ready to do this before a Church of Christ who will not be offended with them, but bless God for what they shall hear. The Presbyterian (i) Ministers of *London* say well, whose words are these, *If Christians are bound to give an account of their Faith and Hope to every one that asketh, yea even to Heathen Persecutors, how much more ought they to do it to the Officers of the Church ? especially at such a Time when they desire to be admitted to such an Ordinance as is not common to all sorts of Christians* I add, And how much more to a whole Church of Christ, if they ask it ? There are also Scripture Examples to encourage this Holy practice. They who were admitted to *Johns Baptism*, made an *Open Declaration* of their Conversion. *Math* 3. 6. And those Converts in *Act.* 2. did manifest that serious desires were wrought in their Souls to be delivered from their Sins, which lay upon their Consciences and pricked their hearts, and that they gladly received the word of promise If this was publickly manifested by them before their Admittance to Baptism ; why should not the like be done now by Christians before their Admission to the Lords Table It is also recorded concerning the Converted *Ephesians*, that they not only believed, but *Came and Confessed. Act.* 19. 18. which implyes *A Publick Declaration of their Conversion*

And

And we find that the Apostle *Paul* was ready upon all just occasions to relate the story of his Conversion.   This does warrant Christians now to practice the like on just occasions. And consequently when a Church of Christ shall call for it.   The great *Austin* in his Book of Confessions, relates the story of his Conversion : The like we find in the published lives of many Saints.   *Justin Martyr* in his disputation with *Tryphon* the Jew giveth a Marvellous account of his Conversion, by means of a Reverend old man, that advised him to Read the Scriptures and to pray to God for illumination, and then departed out of his sight.

2. It is necessary that Churches should know that those whom they admit to their Communion are duely qualified for that Communion.   That they have in them (so far as men are able to judge) that which is the matter of Self-Examination, *viz. Faith* and *Repentance.* That they have an ability to Examine themselves, and not only Doctrinally but Spiritually *to discern the Lords Body.* 1 *Cor.* 11. 28, 29. Now one way for the Church to know that they are such, is, by a *Relation of Experiences*   Nor can it be known except by a *Relation,* or that which shall be *Equivalent* thereunto; as our worthy (*k*) Mr *Mitchel* has Evinced.

3. This practice of our Churches has a tendency to promote *Godliness in the Power*

of

(*k*) *See his Life. p.* 84.

of it. I bless the Lord, in that there are at this day in *London,* several *Religious Societies* of the *Communion of the Church of England,* whose design is to promote Religion in the Power of it. Now these Societies require of such as joyn to them, that they *give the Society a Solemn account of their sence of Spiritual things,* which they do sometimes Orally and sometimes in Writing. One that has perused some of their Papers, Reports that they have in them such Pious and sensible Expressions as would mightily affect any Pious Person to read them. But of this I have made a more large Recitation in a lately (1) published *Epistle.* Now since this practice has a tendency to promote Godliness, why should it not be continued in our Churches? If the *Reformers in the Church of England,* require a Solemn account of their sence of Spiritual things of those that are Admitted into their *Religious Societies,* why may not we require the like of them that joyn to ou Churches, which are *Religious Societies?*

4. This practice has been and will be attended with blessed effects.

For,

1. It will cause the Name of God to be glorified. The Church that Heareth a Savoury *Relation* from any that present themselves to their Communion, will praise God for his Grace in them. *Gal.* 1. 24.

2. The

(1) *See my Epistle before Mr.* Willards *Sermons on* 2 Tim 3 5.

2. The Lords people will have Joy and Comfort in such Members being added to them. If *Paul* and *Barnabas* did cause great joy to the Brethren *by declaring the Conversion of others. Act* 15 3. That Christian will cause great joy to a whole Church of Christ, that shall *Relate* to them, the Experience which he has had of the Grace of God in his own Conversion. It is good to be a helper and not an hinderer of the joy of Saints. 2 *Cor.* 1. 24.

3. The person that does thus joyn himself to the Lords People will have more of their Love and Affection than could otherwise be expected. When they perceive what Experience he has had of the Converting Grace of God in his Soul, every one that is Godly will Love him, and their Hearts will be United to him. 1 *Joh.* 5. 1. I Appeal to the Children of God if they do not find it thus. If when they hear any persons make a very Experimental Relation of Gods dealings with them, in Convincing them of their misery by Nature, and bringing them to cast themselves upon Christ, and helping them against special Temptations, they do not find in their hearts a Singular Love and Holy Affection towards such persons ever after that day. From such Considerations as these mentioned, the practice of the Churches of *New-England* respecting the matter in Question is to be Justifyed, and I pray God, that it may be with due Solemnity continued. That some

D

of our Presbyterian Brethren require that which is equivalent to what is with us called a *Publick Relation*, of those whom they admit to the Lords Supper, is to be seen by a Discourse, called, *The Young mans claim to the Sacrament*, Written by my worthy Friend Mr. *John Quick*, a Reverend Minister now in *London*. I shall only add, that care is to be taken, Lest this custom of the Churches *degenerate into a meer Forma'ity*. Not only things in themselves Lawful and Good, but the Holy Institutions of Christ, have through the Malice of Satan and the Corruptions of men, been turned into *Formalities*. So are Church-officers, Sacraments, and Church-censures in the *Church of Rome*, and in some Protestant Churches also ; which are not throughly cleansed from the Romish Superstitions. Our *Customary Relations* may and will be so too, if we be not careful to prevent it. Insipid, Sapless *Relations* which are used only *Proforma*, will not Edify ; but give Scandal, and Prejudice many against this Laudable Practice. There are Reports, as if in some Churches, Persons have brought *written Relations* first to the Minister, and then to the Church, which were not of their own dictating, but devised by others for them. I hope these Reports have nothing of Truth in them, but if they have, I am sure that such *Lyars to the Holy Ghost*, have Exceedingly provoked the Lord.

QUES-

QUESTION. V.

HAS the Church Covenant as Commonly practised in the Churches of New England, any Scripture Foundation ?

Answ. This *Question* was Considered at a General Convention of Ministers at *Boston,* May 26. 1698. And all the Ministers then present (one only excepted) did Concur in the *Affirmative.* The Reasons to prove that this Practice of our Churches is not an humane Invention, but grounded on the Word of God, are such as these.

1. Nothing is more Indisputable then that under the Old Testament, the Church was Constituted by a Covenant. Nor was any Proselyte admitted into that Church, but by laying hold of the Covenant. A Proselyte was *Filius fæderis* a *Son of the Covenant.* The Jews were *Unchurched* by being *Discovenanted.* *Zech.* 11 10. Things abundantly insisted on in the Old Testament, are more sparingly mentioned in the New. Such as the Sanctification of the Sabbath, and the Church State of the Infant Children of the Lords People. The like may be said as to the Church Covenant. Several Eminent Divines have given this reason why the Word *Covenant* is not mentioned by the Apostles, when they speak of particular Churches. *viz.* Because it is founded

on

on moral Equity, and often mentioned in the Old Testament. Moreover (as is noted by a Learned Author) the name *Covenant* and *Covenanting*, was that which would have made the Churches in those dayes Obnoxious to the Civil Powers, who were then Enemies to Christianity. Therefore the Apostles did forbear the *Names*, but Established the *Thing* by Similitudes evidently implying it.

2. Scriptures which relate to Gospel Times, intimate such a Covenant as is used in our Churches. *Isa.* 62. 5. 'Tis said of the Churhes, *Thy Sons shall Marry thee*, which implies a Covenant. Thus *Isa* 44. 5 *One shall say I am the Lords, and another shall Subscribe with his hand unto the Lord, and Surname himself by the name of Israel.* This is Explicit Covenanting, to be in Gospel Times So *Isa.* 56 4. *They that chuse the things that please me, and take hold of my Covenant.*

3. Members in particular Evangelical Churches are said to be *Fellow Citizens*. *Eph.* 2. 19 Now there is no Admission into *jus Civitatis*, or City priviledges, but by an Act which implies a Covenant. Citizens are in a Covenant together to keep the Laws, and maintain the Liberty of the City.

4 A Church when *Collapsed*, is restored by a *Renovation* of their Church *Covenant* with God, and with one another : Of which we have Instances in the Scripture. 2 *Chron.* 23. 16. and 29. 9, 10. and 34 31, 32. *Ezra.* 10.

10. 3, 5. *Nehe.* 10. 29. Now there is the same reason of *Restitution*, as of *Institution.*

5 Nothing else can be mentioned as Constituting a Particular Church, but only a *Covenant, Agreement,* or *Consent* to walk with God and one another according to the Rules of the Gospel. Meer *Cohabitation* does not make a Church Member, for then Jews and Pagans would be Members of Evangelical Churches. Nor does Profession do it, for then it would be impossible to cut off Scandalous Members by *Excommunication.* Nor *Baptism:* For then upon the ceasing of Membership in a Particular Church, a man must be rebap ised

6 There are Scriptures in the New-Testament which imply such a Covenant, as that which we plead for. *Act* 2 42. *They Continued,* The Greek word signifies, *They joyned and Cleaved together.* So *Act.* 5. 13. None durst *Joyn themselves, i. e.* give themselves to the Church; they were afraid of being Married to the Church The word is the same with that *Matth.* 19. 6 It is in respect of the Covenant (as Dr. *Goodwin* (m) observes) that they who are Conjugally related, are said to be joyned together.

7. If *Implicit Covenanting* is absolutely necessary to the being of a particular Church, than *Explicit Covenanting* must needs be a good thing. The more Explicit men are in Confessing Christ, and owning his Institutions, the

D 3

(m) In his 4th Vi'un.

the more do they Glorify him. *Matth* 10.33,
Mark 8. 39 There is (as Mr. (*n*) *Stone* the
famous Teacher of *Hartford* has obſerved)
*much of the Viſible Glory of Chriſt appearing in
the Explicitneſs of the Church Covenant, when
men viſibly bind themſelves and their Chidren to
Chriſt.* That *Explicit Covenanting* was practiſed among Chriſtians in the next ages to the
Apoſtles, is Evident from *Pliney* (who lived
Anno. 110) his Letter to the Emperor *Trajan.*
Having Enquired into what was *Cuſtomary*
in *Chriſtian Aſſemblies,* He ſayes that they did
meet to Worſhip Chriſt, and that they did
by an Oath bind themſelves to attend the *Diſcipline,* that they would not allow of Adulteri s,
Thefts, Lying, or any Evil thing to be a-
mong them. We ſee in *Juſtin Martyr,* his
Second Apology (who lived within fifty Years of
ſome of the Apoſtles) that Chriſtians were in
thoſe Dayes admitted into Church Fellowſhip,
declared their Reſolution in all things to Con-
form to the Word of God They did not
only profeſs their belief of the Chriſtian Religion, but promiſed to live accordingly. Apol.
2. p. 93, 94. *Tertullian* (*o*) in his *Apology* ſpeaking of *Plinies* Letter but now cited, Expreſſ-
eth the Practice of thoſe Primitive Chriſtians,
by ſaying that they met together *ad Confede-
randam Diſciplinam,* which ſhows that they
had both a *Diſcipline* and a *Covenant* amongſt
them, and clearly Explaines the meaning of
                                                    Plinies

(*n*) *In his Anſwer to Mr Hudſon. p* 41.
     (*o*) *Cap.* 2. *p.* (*Mihi*) 13.

Plinies Sacrament or Oath, which he affirms to be Practised in the Christian Assemblies. *Commenius (p)* informs us that in the *Bohemian* Churches such as were admitted to full Communion, made a publick profession of their Faith before the whole Church, withall promising to live according to the rules of the Gospel.   In the beginning of Queen *Eliz.* Reign, several Congregations in *England*, particularly those in *Coventry*, and in *Northampton*, did publickly profess Repentance for their Idolatry, and *Promised* Obedience to the Protestant Doctrine then restored and established; which Mr *Robinson* in his Answer to Mr. *Bernard, p.* 464. Supposeth to be the deed not of the whole Congregations, but of some Ministers, a few of their people joyning with them. There are some who say that *Presbyterians* are against *Explicit Covenanting:*   My design is to vindicate them as well as their *Congregational Brethren.*   And I must therefore say, that such an Imputation to them all, is an injurious Reflection. Both the one & the other acknowledge that *Explicit Covenanting* is not *Essential* to the being of a *Particular Church.*   Nevertheless, that it is very useful to the *bene esse* thereof, for the more effectual Management of Discipline, and preservation of Order in the Churches, which renders it a duty.   Dr. *Hornbeck* (a Learned professor in the University of *Leyden* who has written in Defence of the

Pres-

(p) *Histor. p.* 46 *et in rat. ordin* p 43, 46.

Presbyterian Government) (†) declares his approbation of the practice of Congregational Churches as to that of *Explicit* Covenanting, and that he approveth of what Mr. *Cotton*, Mr. *Richard Mather*, and Mr. *Norton*, (all of *New-England*) have published on that Subject. The Churches in *Holland* are under the Presbyterian form of Government. It is certain that they did many years since require *Explicit* Covenanting both with God and with the Church, by those that were admitted into their Communion. *Zepperus* who himself was one of them, writes that their manner and order, is, (*q*) *That when any persons are admitted to the Lord's Table, they make a Pub'ick Profession of their Faith before all the Church, and likewise promise and Covenant that they will continue in that Faith, and lead their Lives accordingly.* This personal Covenanting with God and the Church is required by several of the *Synods* in *Holland*, and is highly approved of by the most Learned *Voetius* in his Books of (*r*) *Ecclesiastical Polity.* An *Episcopalian* near upon an hundred years since, complained that the *Calvinists* and Reformed Churches in *France* would not admit any one unto the Lords Table, Except he did make a *Pub'ick Profession of his Faith,* and did also *Promise by the help of God to continue stedfast therein.* Our
Re

(†) *In Epist. ad Dureum. p* 309, 310.
(*q*) *Zepper. de polit. Eccles L. 1. c. 14,*
(*r*) *Part 1. Lib. 1 c. 4.*

Renowned Mr. *Robert Parker*, (who being driven out of *England* by the then Persecuting Prelates lived amongst the Reformed Churches abroad) acquaints us that in those Churches, *When any person seeks Admittance into Church Communion, the Name of him who desires to be a Church Member is Published in the Congregation, that if any one has ought to Object against the Person Propounded, he shou'd acquaint the Elders therewith. If nothing is brought in against him, he is admitted, but not without a Solemn Covenant with God and the Church ; and to the Church he promiseth to walk as becomes that Holy Fellowship, that he will submit to the Discipline of the Church, that he will Watch over the Brethren of that Communion according to the command of Christ.* If (saith Mr *Parker*) (s) this were practised in the *Church of England*, there would be no cause for *A. B. Whitgift* to say, that *the Visible Church is full of Idolaters, Adulterers, Drunkards, and Atheists.* That none were admitted to be Members of Particular Churches amongst the Reformed in (t) *France* without Publick Covenanting or Promising Subjection to the Discipline of Christ, is well known. Now let us hear what a later Presbyterian sayes about an *Explicit Church Covenant* : The Reverend Mr. *Baxter* in his Book called *Church Concord* (n) declares that there

(s) *De pol Eccles.* L. 3. c. 16 p. 171, 172.
(t) See Mr. *Quicks Synodicon.* An. 1565 p 61.
(n) P. 20, 21.

there is no difference at all between the Learned of both perſwaſions. (*Viz.* Presbyterian
and Congregational) about this controverſy.
*The thing (ſayes he) that, the Presbyterian
have ſtood upon is no more but to Vindicate the
Truth of our Churches againſt the Separatiſts
that have denyed them to be true Churches, becauſe they have not an Explicit Covenant. The
deny not but that ſuch a Covenant may con-
duce to the well being of the Church.* And
*he adds further ; I conclude that whatſoever
ſome Particular Perſons may be Guilty of, there
is no real differance between the Presbyterian
and Indepandants in the point of Church Covenant. God forbid, that any faithful Miniſter of
Chriſt ſhould fight againſt that which is profitable to the well-being of the Church, meerly becauſe without it the Church may have a being
Then muſt we plead for hunger and want, and
calamitous diſeaſes that leave us but the being
of men. Nature, and Scripture, and the Pre-
ſidents in the Old Teſtament, and the Doctrin
of the Apoſtles, and the Ancient practice of the
Churches do ſatiſfy us of the uſefulneſs of Holy
Covenants, prudently, ſeriouſly, and ſeaſonably
made.* Thus Mr *Baxter* who has much more
to the ſame purpoſe in his Book of Confirmation.

QUESTION. VI.

IS Publick Reading of the Scriptures without any Explication or Exhortation therewith, part of the work incumbent on a Minister of the Gospel

Answ. The Question is not whether such Readings are Lawful, (for who doubts that) but whether the Minister that shall omit them does fail in that which is some part of his duty. To which the Answer must be *Negative.* It cannot be proved that that which some call *Dumb Reading,* or publick Reading of the Scriptures without any Explication or Exhortation is part of the Pastoral Office, or that which every Minister of the Gospel is bound unto. Some have thought (w) that when *Paul* sayes to *Timothy, Till I come give attendance to Reading,* that he means Publick Reading of the Scriptures; but then he adds, *and to Exhortation and Doctrine.* 1 Tim 4. 13 The Reading of one Chapter with a brief Explication, will Edify the Congregation more than the bare Reading of Twenty Chapters will do. And every Minister should attend that which will be most to the Edification of his People. If publick Reading without Explication or Exhortation therewith is a duty, than those Ministers who when they Read publickly

ly

(w) *V. Dido. clav. p.* 533. *And Aynsworth against* Smith. *p.* 44.

ly do alwayes Expound or Exhort therewith, but do not practice that which is called *Dumb Reading*, are guilty of Sin, as omiting
that which is their duty. But such Ministers
are not guilty of Sin: And if not, it will then
follow that they who practice Reading without Explication under the notion of a duty,
are guilty of Superstition, in making that a
duty which is none. As for *Reading* without
Interpretation, there are many who can do
that as well as the Minister. We find in *Neh.*
8. 8. *That they read in the Book of the Law
distinctly, and gave the sence, and caused them to
understand the Reading.* That the Jews were
wont to Read the Scriptures in their *Synagogues*
every Sabbath day, we all know. The *Pen-
teteuch* (or five Books of *Moses*) was by them
divided into fifty four *Parashoth*, or *Sections*,
which they read over once every year.
When *Antiochus* inhibited the Reading of *the
Law*, the Jews instead thereof Read *the Prophets*; after which it became customary to
Read both of them. The Jews called the
Lections out of the Prophets, *Haphtharot*,
which signifies *Dismission*, because they were
wont to dismiss their Assemblies with those
Readings But that *Explications* and *Exhor-
tations* used to attend their *Readings* is certain.
It belonged to him that was the *chief Ruler* of
the *Synagogue* to see this done, who did sometimes permit others to do it. The chief
man in the *Synagogue* was by the Jews called
Chazzan, i. e. the Inspector, or *Overseer*, and
some-

sometimes they called him *Sheliach Tsibbor, i. e. The Angel of the Congregation.* The work of this person was to go before the Congregation in prayer. And although he did seldome read himself, he appointed others to do it, making his choice of Seven, and diligently observed how they read. This *Overseer of the Synagogue,* or some other person used to *Interpret* what was read. On this very account, the *Synagogue* was called, *Beth Midrash,* i. e. *The House of Exposition.* See Mr. *Weems Exercitation.* 15. p. 163. Where he shows that it was the manner of the Jews after the reading of the Law and the Prophets to Expound. Besides what Writers on this Subject inform us, the thing is clear from these Scriptures. 2 *Chron.* 17 9: *Luk* 4. 16.····22. *Act.* 13. 15. and 15. 21. It cannot be proved that Reading without *Explication* or *Application* was used by the Pastors in the Churches of Christians in *Apostolical* Times, nor yet in the next Ages to them. We see in *Justin Martyr,* that the Scriptures were then Read, but a Sermon thereon followed. In *Cyprians* (x) Time there was a *Reader* distinct from the *Presbyter,* who was Ordained to that Office. He is by *Cyprian* called *Doctor Audientium,* (which as the most Learned Professor of *Utrick* has observed) implies that he did more than barely Read. In *Austins* time, they used to have *three Lections.* They read an *Epistle,* and

E   some-

(x) *V. Cyprian Epist.* 24. & 34.

something out of the *Gospel*, and a *Psalm*, after which the Minister Preached upon what was read. Therefore *Austin* begins some of his Sermons with saying, *Tres has Lectiones*, &c. *These three Readings which you have heard* &c. When the distinction of *Libri proto-Canonici et deutero-canonici* was received, the Reading of the Scriptures in Publick Congregations brought in the Reading of *Apochrypha-Books*, (and at last the Reading of *Homilies* instead of Preaching) which is still practised in *Popish*, and in some Protestant Congregations, notwithstanding there is in the *Council* of *Laodicea* a *Canon* against it. From these and the like Considerations *Publick Readings* of the Scriptures unless with some *Exposition* thereon was not practised in the Churches of *New-England* by those Eminent Servants of Christ, who first planted Churches in this Wilderness. Mr. *Rutherford* in his account of the Government of the Church of *Scotland*, under that head of *The Pastors Duty*, (*p.* 314) mentions reading Scriptures with Exposition, but says nothing of reading without that.   I am informed that there are Congregations in *Scotland*, where not the *Pastor*, but the *Ruling Elder* readeth the Scripture.   Mr. *Calderwood*, (that Learned Scotch Divine who goes under the name of *Didoclavius*) sayes, that he would not have Sermons without reading the Scriptures : Nor reading without Interpretation. *Non probo Lectionem sine Interpretatione. Altare*

tare. Damascan. p. 632. In some (y) Congregations in *Germany,* the Scriptures have been read in order, and illustrated with a brief and pious Explication. In the *Tigurin Liturgy,* there is no mention of Reading without Interpretation. I therefore suppose that there is no such practice in the *Helvetian* Churches. I knew an Eminent Minister in *England* who did for many years read the Scriptures in the publick Congregation, without any Explication, but in his latter Time he saw cause to alter his Judgement and practice therein, alwayes joyning Interpretation with his Reading. The *Bishop* of *Derry* in his late discourse of *Humane Inventions in the worship of God,* makes a sad complaint, that the *Nonconformist* dont use to read the Scriptures in their Assemblies. He sayes, that *in all the Meetings in the North of Ireland in a whole year there is not so much Scripture read as in one day in the Church. Sure it is a sad thing* (sayes he) *that a man may go to most Meetings many years, and never hear one entire Chapter read in them.* Mr. *Boyse* Answers him, that *it is the general practice of the Ministers in the North of Ireland* (the Ministers there are generally of the Scotch Nation, and of the Presbyterian Judgement) *to read every Morning an entire portion of Scripture, usually a whole Chapter, or at least so much as they can go through with, in an Exposition of half an hours length.* 'Now

E 2 'let

(y) *V. Voet. de pol. Ecclef part.* 1. *lib.* 2 *p.* 605.

' let us suppose there are Forty Meetings in
' the North of *Ireland*, and that in each Meet-
' ing half a Chapter is read every Lords-day,
' for three quarters of the year, by this Com-
' putation, there will be near Eight hundred
' Chapters read in these Meetings in a year.
' But will the Bishop perswade us that there
' is as much read in one day in the Parish
' Church. Mr. *Boyse* moreover sayes, that
' there are few Sermons of the *Dissenters* in
' which there is not as much of the *Scriptures*
' recited to the people as if put together would
' make up two or three Chapters And that
' the *Dissenters* have better reason to blame
' the *Conforming Clergy* for casting out the
' Exposition of Scripture when read (as that
' Exercise is distinguished from Sermons) then
' the Bishop to reproach them for not reading
' the Scripture. And that those more fully
' comply with Gods Command, who read
' and Expound, than those that only read.
' He takes notice what a miserable sort of
' Clergy there is in *Russia* and other parts of
' the Christian World, where their Ministers
' are meer Readers. Thus Mr. *Boyse* a worthy Minister of the Presbyterian Judgment
in *Dublin*, whom I have the rather taken notice of because he was born in *New-England*,
at *Rowley*, in which Church his Father (a man
of Eminent piety) was an Officer. To conclude the answer to the Question before us.
It is evident that in *Origens* time Interpretation
of the Scripture did accompany the publick
Reading

Reading of it. For he calls their Sermons, *Diageseis*, (†) the enarrations or *Explication* of what had been *Read*. *Origen* was wont himself to read several Chapters. We find that he read the 25, 26, 27, 28. Chapters of the First Book of *Samuel* at one time, but deferred the Exposition of the last of those Chapters to another Opportunity. At another time he read in *Jeremiah* from Verse 10. of Chapter 15. to Verse 5. of Chapter 17. and spent an hour (as he was wont to do) in Explaining and Applying what he had read. As for those who are of the Bishops mind, that many Presbyterians as well as Congregational men are guilty of Sin, and *Humane Invention in the worship of God*, in that they alwayes add Explication or Application to what they read in publick I shall only recommend to their serious Consideration two passages, both which are quoted by Mr. *Boyse*. One is that of *Austin, Quare Legitur, si Silebitur, aut quare auditur, si non Exponitur* : Why do we publickly read the Scripture, if we must be silent and not Expound it. The other is that of *Bernard, Non tradit Mater parvulo nucem integram, sed frangit eam et nucleum porrigit* : Opening the Scripture is like taking the Kernel out of the Nut.

(†) *Contra Celsum*. L. 3. p. 142.

QUESTION. VII.

IS Baptism to be Administred to all Children, whom any Professed Christian shall ingage to see Educated in the Christian Religion?

Answ. If the Question were only whether all Children Adopted by Believing Parents might not be Baptised; we should not oppose. For this is granted not only by the generality of *Protestant Divines*, but Eminent Writers of the *Congregational Perswasion*, particularly Dr. *Ames*, and Mr. *Cotton*, are for the *Affirmative*. But as the *Question* is worded, we defend the *Negative*. And say, that all such persons as are Comprehended in the Question, have not a right to Baptism, consequently it would be a *Profanation* of the Holy Institution of Christ to Administer Baptism to them.   For,

1. *Papists, Socinians* and other Hereticks are *Professed Christians*. But their Children ought not to be Baptised For that is to declare their *Religion* to be the true Religion. When the Children of *Israel* were *Baptised unto Moses* in the Cloud, it was thereby signifyed that the Religion taught by *Moses*, was the true Religion. 1 *Cor* 10. 2 But *Papists* have corrupted the very Essentials of the true Christian Religion, not by one but by many Heresies by them mentained besides their Idolatry. Nor does it follow that

that if the Children of Papifts had no right to *Baptifm*, that then their Baptifm was a *Nullity* and muft be Iterated. For they baptife in the fame Name, and ufe the fame outward Element (though with Superftitious Additions of their own) which is of Divine Inftitution; in which refpects although *Fieri non debuit, factum valet*. Now if the Children of *Papifts* notwithftanding their being *Profeffed Chriftians*, have no right to Baptifm; if *any* fuch fhould ingage to fee a Child Educated in the Chriftian Religion, that could not Entitle him to this Sacred Ordinance. Who can believe that if a Papift will undertake to be the *God-Father* of the Spurious Children of *Negroes* or *Indians*, then thefe Children ought to be Baptifed ? But they ought to be fo, if this be a true *Pofition, That Baptifm ought to be Adminiftred to all Children whom any Profeffed Chriftian fhall ingage to fee Educated in the Chriftian Religion*. Our firft *Reformers* were large enough in their Principles and Practice as to *the Subject of Baptifm*. Neverthelefs, they taught that the Children of Papifts had no right to Baptifm. So (a) *Calvin, Farel, Beza*. Yea, the (b) *Reformed* Churches in *France* will not admit the Children of Papifts to Baptifm, although Proteftant God fathers would engage for their Education in the true Religion. Our famous Mr. *Carthwrighe*

(a) *V Calvini Epift.*
(b) *See their difcipline G. Lt. Reques*
p. 201.

wright has (e) proved that such Children
have no right to Baptism because they are
cut off from the Covenant, and do not belong to the Visible Church. We must of
necessity own the Church of *Rome* to be a
true Church, if we own the Members of it
to have right to Baptism. But the contrary
has been evinced by Dr. *Whitaker, Alting,
Turretin,* and many others who have made it
appear that Papists only retain the words of
that-which is called the *Apostles Creed,* but not
the true sense of it.

2. There are many professors of *the Protestant* which is the true *Christian Religion,*
whose Children have not by the appointment of Christ any right to Baptism. For we
may not Baptise the Children of profane
Parents. A national Synod in *Holland,* Anno
1619. Permits none to be *Susceptors* in Baptism, but such as are Orthodox in Religion,
and *of a blameless Life.* The *Ecclesiastical
Discipline* of the Reformed Churches in *France,*
permits not them who are suspended from the
Lords Supper, to present their Children to
Baptism as long as their Suspension shall en-
dure. Every body knows that *Nil dat quod
non habet.* No man that has not a right to
Baptism himself, can convey a right to his
Children. The *Primitive* right must be as
good

(e) *In* 1 *Reply* p. 172, 173 &
2d. *part of* 2 *Reply* p. 142.
(f) *V. Voet. pol. Eccles.* part 1:
L. 2. p. 661.

good as the *Derivative*.   But a *Known wicked man* has no right to the Seals of Gods Covenant. *Pfal.* 50. 16, 17. It is a dishonour to the Name of Christ that such shou'd be owned as his Servants, or wear the *Livery* that belongs to such. 2 *Tim.* 2. 19. When the Church is made an Inn to receive all Comers by a Promiscuous Baptism, the Name of the Lord is prophaned, as sayeth our great (g) *Carthwright* but now mentioned. The Ancient Doctors, particularly (h) *Tertullian* (i) *Chryfoftom,* and Especially *Auftin,* (k) (who has largely disputed against the Baptifing of Ungodly men though Profeffed Chriftians) are wont to alledge that Scripture. *Matth.* 7. 6: *Give ye not that which is Holy to Dogs,* against the Baptifing of such persons : which words notwithftanding they have another sense are fitly applyed here. For *Baptifm* is an *Holy thing.* And the Scripture compares wicked men (though Profeffors of the true Religion) unto *Dogs. Pfal.* 22 20 2 *Pet.* 2 22. No man thinks that Infidels ought to be Baptised   But *Practical Infidels* are many times worfe than *Profeffed* ones. 1 *Tim.* 5 8: *If any man provide not for his own Houfe, he has denyed the Faith, and is worfe then an Infidel.* Many *Profeffed Chriftians* do *practically deny the Faith;* by their Vicious Lives they
Nul-

(g) *Defence of Admonition. p.* 137.
(h) *De Baptifimo. c* 18.
(i) *De Compunction Cordis L.* I.
(k) *De Fide et operibus.*

Nullify their Christianity, and are worse than Infidels. To Baptise them would be to profane the Sacred and Glorious Name of Christ. Shall Swearers, Drunkards, Fornicators, and such like, who live in the visible breach of *the Everlasting Covenant* every Day, have that Covenant Sealed unto them by *Baptism*, when it is manifest that they have no Interest in the thing Signifyed and Sealed by that Ordinance ? Have Excommunicates or their Children a right to Baptism ? The Jews (as *Buxtorf* (*l*) observes) looked upon Infant Children as Excommunicate with the Parents And therefore (as another Learned Author informs us) such Children were not Circumcised. A National Synod in *Scotland*, *Anno* 1560, has declared that the Children of Excommunicate Parents ought not (until the Parent Manifest Repentance) to be admitted unto Baptism. *Beza* allows of it in case the Children of the Excommunicate be by the Parents committed to the Tuition and Education of a faithful Member of the Church, (*m*) as we see in his Letter to the Ministers of *Newenburg* in *Switzerland*, but not without that Caution. When in *Geneva* a Protestant Member of a Church there had Apostatized to the Popish Religion, the Grandmother remaining still a Member of the true Church, desired Baptism

(*l*) *Buxtorf. in Lexic. Thalmudic. pag.* 1101. *Godwin Moses & Aaron. B.* 5. *Ch.* 2.
(*m*) *Beza Epist.* 10.

Baptism for her Grand-child ; but considering that the next Parents were both of them Idolaters, and the Child remaining under their Education, the Renowned *Farel (n)* refused to Baptize it, though his Colleaque would do it, which occasioned an unhappy Schism in that Church. But then shall persons who are *ipso Jure (i e. Visolius Legis sine sententia judicis)* Excommunicate (which is to be affirmed of many *Professed Christians)* by Baptism be declared to have a regular standing in the Visible Church ? It is by some pretended, that *Presbyterians* are for Baptizing *all Professed Christians.* They that say so are injurious to those our worthy Brethren. The Great *John Calvin* has been Esteemed the Father of Presbyterians. He was not for Baptizing all that pretended to Christianity, as his *(o)* Epistles show. In the year 1550. Our English *Josiah,* King *Edward* the Sixth granted to the *Dutch* Protestants, and other Strangers in *London,* a Charter of Incorporation to become a Church, and to have a Meeting House for them, and for their Successors, which He Ordained to be called by the name of the *Church of the Lord Jesus, (p)* Enjoyning all his Subjects to permit them *quietly to use and exercise their own proper Rites and peculiar Discipline notwithstanding they*

(n) V. Calvin Epist. 147.
(o) V. Epist. 136.
(p) Fullers Church History,
    B. 7. p. 407.

they agreed not with the Rites and Ceremonies used in the Church of *England.* These Protestants diſſenting from the Church of *England* have been called *Presbyterians.* Their firſt and *noble Paſtor, John,* who was a free Baron of *Laſco* in *Poland,* has Publiſhed an account of their Diſcipline, wherein He declares, *That Baptiſm is Adminiſtred in the Publick Aſſembly of the Church after the Publick Sermon; for ſeeing Baptiſm does ſo belong to the whole Church, that none ought to be driven back that is a Member of the Church, nor to be Adminiſtred to any who is not a Member of it : it is meet that it ſhould be performed Publickly in the face of the whole Church. ---- We do Baptize their Infants alone who have Joyned themſelves to our Church by Publick Confeſſion of their Faith and Obſervation of the Eccleſiaſtical Diſcipline. ---- We ſuffer no Stranger to offer his Infant to Baptiſm in our Church, who has not made a Publick Profeſſion of his Faith, and willingly ſubmitted himſelf to the Diſcipline of our Church.* Thus writes *John a Laſco,* a noble *Polander,* who is Succeeded by the *Dutch Miniſters,* and Church now in *London.* To proceed. The *Leyden* Divines, *Polyander, Rivet, Waleus, Thyſius,* were accounted *Presbyterians.* But they were not for Baptizing *profeſſed Chriſtians* whoſe Lives were profane. They (*q*) ſay expreſly; *Si quis vero Licet fidem Profeſſus impie vivat Baptiſmo initiandus non eſt,* for which they give this Reaſon,

(*q*) *Synops. pur. Relig. diſp.* 44. *Theſ.* 46.

Reason, That Baptism is a Sacrament not only of Faith, but of Repentance ; For which cause they that persist Impenitently in any Scandalous practises are not subjects meet for that Sacrament. The Learned *Spanheimius* is called a *Presbyterian.* But he has by weighty Reasons proved, that Profane men though Profess'd Christians, ought not to be Baptised. Mr *Baxter* goes for a *Presbyterian.* (r) He has by irrefragable Arguments evinced, that *the Children of notoriously Ungodly men* ought not to be Baptised. Mr. *George Gilaspy* was a Presbyterian of the Church in *Scotland.* Now his words are these. *(t) I believe* (saith he) *no Conscientious Minister would adventure to Baptise one who has manifest and Infallible Signs of Irregeneration. Surely we cannot be answerable to God if we shou'd Administer Baptism to a man whose works and words do manifestly declare him to be an Unregenerate Unconverted person.* By the Testimonies which have been cited, it is clear that the denial of Baptism to some who are professed Christians is not the Principle of *Independents* only.

3. Such Laxness in the Administration of Baptism as is Expressed in the Question before us, is Popish and Antichristian. It was not so in the Primitive Ages of Christianity. That Error of *the necessity of Baptism* (not only

F

neces-

(r) *In his disputations of Right to Sacraments,*
(t) *In Aarons Rod. p.* 515

necessitate præcepti sed medij) in order to Salvation. Likewise that Error of *Baptismal Regeneration*, that Baptism does Regenerate men *Ex opere operato*, as Popish Authors teach, brought in this Error also. *Bellarmine*, and others of that Religion affirm that Baptism doe *Sanctify the Unclean*, and that therefore it i not profaned when administred to person known to be wicked. *In pursuance* of this pria ciple a Popish Priest Baptised no less than three hundred thousand *Americans.* (*u*) And another Seven hundred thousand as their own Historians inform us) amongst all which there was not one Good Christian. Most certainly, the Apostles did not Baptise after that Lax manner. And *John Baptist* requir ed *Fruits meet for Repentance* of the Adult per sons whom he admitted to this Sacred Ordi nance ; and when a *Generation of Vipers* came to him for Baptism, he rejected them because of their Impenitency. *Matth* 3. 8. with *Luk.* 7. 3 0.

(u) *V. Purchase pilgr. concerning*
America. p. 115

QUESTION. VIII.

IS *Baptism in a private House where there is no Church Assembly allowable ?*

Answ. Papists, Episcopal Protestants, and some *Lutherans* plead for it. But the

(*a*)

(*a*) Doctrine of the old *Waldenses* was, that *Baptiſm ought to be Adminiſtred in a full Congregation, to the end that he that is received into the Church, ſhou'd be reputed & held of all for a Chriſtian Brother, & that all the Congregation might pray for him, that he may be a Chriſtian in Heart, as he is outwardly eſteemed a Chriſtian.* Moſt of our Writers (eſpecially *Presbyterians*) diſapprove of *Private Baptiſm* The *Reformed* in *France,* (*b*) & the Churches in (*c*) *Holland* alſo require Baptiſm to be publickly adminiſtred. Our *Engliſh Presbyterians* in the *Directory*, ſays that *Baptiſm is not to be adminiſtred in private places, or privately, but in the place of publick Worſhip, and in the face of the Congregation.* The *Geneva Divines* (as is to be ſeen in *Zanchys* Epiſtles) when this caſe was propoſed to them, *Whether Baptiſm might not be adminiſtred in private,* Adviſed thoſe that ſent to them, *not to Baptiſe any but where there was a publick Aſſembly,* for which they gave ſeveral Reaſons. *Calvin,* although he does not judge private Baptiſm to be a meer nullity, neverthelſs in his (*c*) *Inſtitutions,* he diſallows of it. And in his *Epiſtles,* he reaſoneth after

F 2   this

(*a*) *See* Perin *of the Waldenſes* Doctrine. p. 43.

(*b*) *See their diſcipline* ch. 11. s 6.

(*b*) *v. Voet. de pol. Eccleſ. part* 1. L. 2 p. 726.

(*c*) L. 4. c. 15. s. 16.

this manner, (d) *Baptism Seals our Introduction and Initiation into the Visible Church and Body of Christ, and our Adoption to the Heavenly Inheritance,* therefore (sayes *Calvin*) *Fas non est administrare Baptismum nisi in Cœtu Publico,* It is not lawful to administer Baptism except in a publick Congregation. The Judicious and Learned Professors (e) of *Leyden,* condemn private Baptisms : So does (f) *Maresius,* and so does (g) *Alting.* In *Scotland,* (h) Mr. *Calderwood,* (i) Mr. *Gelaspy,* (k) Mr. *Rutherford,* have all of them witnessed against it. It is evident that in the early Ages of Christianity *Private Baptisms* were not used, but there was an Error on the other hand, for they used not to Baptise except at *Easter* and *Pentecost,* when were the greatest Assemblies. In the very beginings of the *Reformation* in *England,* private Baptism was not allowed of except in case of necessity. King *Edward 6.* his *Common Prayer Book,* requires that the people should be admonished to bring their Children to Baptism only on the Lords dayes, and on Holidays, that so all the Congregation might be witnesses of their being received into the

(d) *Epist* 185.
(e) *Syhops. disp.* 44. *Thes* 53.
(f) *In Epist. Theol.*
(g) *Problem. Theol* part. 2. p. 162.
(h) *Altar. damasc.*
(i) *English popish Ceremonies.* p. 142.
(k) *Plea for Presbytery.* p. 315.

the number of the Faithful, and that they might all be put in mind of what they had promiſed in Baptiſm.   And although private Baptiſms are ordinarily practiſed by the Miniſters of the Church of *England*, when no neceſſity compels them, the *Liturgy* allows not of it.   The Arguments which our Divines produce againſt private Baptiſm are ſuch as theſe.

1. John Baptiſt did not Baptiſe in private, but where there was an open Publick meeting. It has been objected that *Paul* Baptiſed the Jaylor in a private Houſe where was no Church Aſſembly : To which is Anſwered, that *Paul* was an extraordinary Officer : And that it was impoſſible in that Place at that Time to call a Congregation of Chriſtians to be witneſſes of the Adminiſtration when as yet there were no Chriſtians in that City.

2. Baptiſm is a part of publick Miniſtry : It ought to be as publick as Preaching. Nor may it be adminiſtred except by one who is called to the Publick Miniſtry.

3. No perſon may be caſt out of the Church privately, but the proceedings therein ought to be publick with the conſent and preſence of the whole Church   Therefore the Seal of Admiſſion into the Church by Baptiſm ought to be publick alſo.   There is a parity of reaſon therein.

4. Our profeſſion of the Name of God and of Chriſt ought to be in the moſt publick way and manner that poſſibly can be. *Matth:*

F 3   1032.

10. 32. *Rev.* 14. 1. But in Baptifm we do in a fingular manner make a profeffion of the Name of the true God and of Jefus Chrift. *Matth.* 28.20. *Act* 19. 5. *Gal.* 3. 27

5. *Didoclavius* (*l*) argues more like a Congregational man than like a Presbyterian. For thus he reafons.   The power of Adminiftring Sacraments is as *Chryfoftom* fpeaks, *Delivered to the Church*, although the Difpenfation or Adminiftration thereof belongs to the Paftors. Now *the Minister alone* (fayes he) *has not all the power, fo as that he may feparately Administer the Sacrament to whom he pleafeth, but there ought to be the approbation, confent, and prefence of the Church.*

6   This practice of private Baptifm was grounded on an Error; namely on a perfwafion of the abfolute neceffity of Baptifm to Salvation.   *Auftin* was not without that Error. He thought that Infants who dyed Unbaptif'd could not go to Heaven, for which reafon he has been called, *Durus Pater Infantum.* There was about the fame time another Error worfe than this crept into many Churches; *viz.* That none could be faved that did not partake of the Lords Supper.   So did they mifunderftand that Scripture *Joh.* 6 53. As it Sacramental Eating were there intended; whereas thofe words were fpoken by our Saviour before the Lords Supper was inftituted, and are meant of the Souls Eating and Drinking by Faith.   But from this Error it

was

(1) *Ubi fupra p.* 854.

was that Children were made to Eat and Drink of the Confecrated Bread and Wine. So left they fhould mifs of Salvation they would Baptifm them in private when it could not be done in publick. But we know that it is the *Contempt*, and not the meer *Privation* of Sacraments that is damning. The *Helvetian* Churches do in no cafe allow of Baptifm in any private Houfe. See the *Liturgy* of the Churches in *Switzerland.* p. 90.

QUESTION. IX.

OUght all that Contribute towards the Maintainance to have the Priviledge of Voting
in the Election of a Paftor ?

Anfw. It would be *Simoniacal* to Affirm that this Sacred Priviledge may be Purcha-fed with Money, or, that *Contribution* can Entitle to it.   For,

1. This is againft the Scripture, and that in more refpects than one.

1. The Scripture requires all that are taught to Contribute to him that is their Teacher. *Gal.* 6. 6. But it does not fay that all who are taught fhall have power to chufe a Paftor for that Church where they are taught. In the Primitives Times the *Catechu-mens* did many of them Contribute to him that was their Inftructor, but not one of
them

them all had the priviledge of Voting in the Election of the Churches Paſtor.

2 The word of God has given power to the Brethren in particular Churches to chuſe their own Officers. *Act.* 1. 26. & 6. 2, 3, 5. & 14 23. Wherefore to give it to others beſides them is not according to the word of Chriſt.

3. If all that Contribute have power to Vote in the Election of a Paſtor, then many women muſt have that Priviledge, for they may Contribute to the Maintainance. But this the Apoſtle allows not of. 1 *Cor.* 14. 34, 35. So that this Affirmation is Contrary to the Scripture in more reſpects then one

2. It is againſt Reaſon. For them who have no right to the Lords Supper themſelves, to appoint who ſhall be the diſpenſer of that Ordinance to others, is highly irrational.

3 This will deprive particular Churches of that Power which does belong to them, and which Chriſt ha's purchaſed for them with the price of his own Blood. To have power to Chuſe their own Paſtors is an invaluable Priviledge. For them to give or rather to ſell that Priviledge away to all that will *Contribute*, muſt needs be diſpleaſing to the Lord who has bought it for them at ſo dear a rate. It may be the *Contributors* will be more than twice ſo many as the Brethren of the Church. So it may eaſily come to paſs, that a Paſtor ſhall be Choſen and not ſo much as one in the Church that did, or could in Conſcience Vote.

ſor

for him. So then this Principle is of Dangerous Confequence. It may foon prove fatal and deftructive to the Churches, and to the Intereft of Chrift amongft them.

4 It is contrary to the principles and practifes of Chriftians in the Primitive Times, *Eufebius* fayes that after the Death of *James*, the Church chofe *Simeon* the Son of *Cleophas* to be his Succeffor. Nothing is more Evident then that in the Fiift ages of the Church, Paftors were Chofen by all and only their Flocks ; in Chufing a Minifter they did *K'erozein*, that is Chufe him by Lot ; from whence it was that Minifters had the name of the *Clergy* given to them. *Ignatius* writing to the Church in *Philadelphia* tells them, that it belonged to them to Chufe their Paftor. The *Nicene Council* in a *Synodal Letter* to the Churhes in *Africa*, advife them to Chufe Orthodox Paftors inftead of *Arians*. *Cyprian* tells us, (w) that *Cornelius* was made Bifhop *Suffragio Plebis*, by the Suffrages of the people. Yea, he fayes Lib. 1. Epift 41. that *Plebs maxime poteftatem habet, vel facerdotes dignos eigendi, vel indignos recufandi*. And there are many paffages in him and other Fathers, (as they are called) which fhew that the power of Chufing *Paftors* was in the Church. Nay, Antichrift had got a confiderable footing in the World, before ever this priviledge of Chufing their own *Paftors* was wreftled out of the hands of *Particular Churches*. It was about the Year 1219. that *Pope Innocent*

(w) *In Epift.* 52.

cent. III. forbid the *Laity* to meddle in the Election of any Church Guide. M *La Roque* (*x*) fuppofeth, that *Canon* was made in oppofition to the *Albigenfes* who retained the Ancient practice of the Churches in Chufing their own Officers. The Emperor *Conftantine* writing to *Nicomedia,* fayes, that it was in their power to make a Choice of what Paftor they pleafed. The Council of *Calcedon* confirms the Churches power of Elections. There are many Inftances to this purpofe in the (*y*) writers of *Ecclefiaftical Hiftory.*

5. All our Great Reformers and Eminent Modern Divines, (Prelatical ones excepted) have afferted the power of Electing Minifters to be in the Church. The depriving the Church of this priviledge is by *Calvin,* called *Impia Ecclefiæ Spoliatio.* A *Spoil* impioufly committed upon the *Church* of God. I could eafily produce Teftimonies for this, out of *Luther, Bullinger, Musculus, Urfin, Junius,* (*z*) & many others but it is needlefs. Some Learned writers of the Presbyterian Judgment, in their arguings againft *Jus Patronatus,* or the power of *Patrons* to impofe Minifters on the people, and in their difputations againft *Epifcopal Inftitution and Induction,* have ftrenuoufly afferted and proved, that *particular Churches have power*

to

(x) *of the Ecclef. difcipline p.* 20.
(y) *v. Theod. l.* 4. *c* 20 *Secrat. l.* 5. *c.* 15. *Zozom. l.* 8. *c.* 19.
(z) *See* Mr. Jacob *of Church Government, with the peoples confent.* Chapt. 3.

to Chuse their own Pastors. One of the Articles agreed unto by the *United Brethren* in *London* is, *That each particular Church ha's right to Chuse their own Officers* That this was the Judgment of the Old *Puritan Nonconformists* is asserted in that Book which bears the Title of *Puritanismus Anglicanus,* which goeth under the name of Dr. *Ames,* because of his preface to it, but Mr. *Bradshaw* and not *Ames* was the Author, as a Learned professor (†) in the University of *Leyden* has informed us.

6 One of our *Synods* in *New England, viz.* that which met at *Boston* in the Year 1662. does Expresly declare, That *the power of Voting in the Church, belongs to Males in full Communion,* and that *others are to be debarred from that Power* Prop. 4. p. 18. In other places of the world, although a *Modest dissenting* is not an offence, yet it is not allowed *in Terms to Contradict,* what has been by Synods Established.

7 To give the Power of Electing Ministers to any besides the particular Churches over which they are set, is Contrary to the Good Laws of this Province, which Confirm unto the *Several Churches therein, all their former Priviledges respecting Divine Worship, and Church Order,* and particularly their Power of Chusing their Ministers, which Laws have (through the Favour of our Lord Jesus Christ to his Churches in *New England*) obtained the *Royal Approbation.* QUES-

(†) *Hornbeck Epist: ad Dureum. p.* 27.

QUESTION X.

IS it Expedient that Churches should enter into a Consociation, or Agreement, that matters of more then ordinary Importance, such as the Gathering of a New Church, the Ordination, Deposition, or Translation of a Pastor be done with Common Consent ?

Answ. This is both Expedient and Necessary. The *Synod* which Convened at *Boston* Anno 1662. ha's sufficiently cleared this Point. And although there was in that *Synod* some dissent as to the *Question* about the *Subject of Baptism* then discussed ; in the Answer to the other *Question* relating to the *Consociation of Churches*, there was an Unanimous Concurrence. The design of which is not (as has *been* well observed by Dr. (*a*) *Ames* and Mr. (*b*) *Parker*) to infringe the Liberty of particular Churches, but from the word of God to direct and strengthen them in the Regular Exercise thereof. The Reasons for it are such as these.

1. The Churches of Christ stand in a Sisterly relation each to other under Christ their head, having the same *Faith*, and ought to have the same *Order*. *Eph* 4 5 *Col.* 2. 5. *Phil.* 3. 16. This Union implyes a suitable Commu-

(a) *Medul. Theol. L.* 1 c 39 *Thes* 27.
(b) *De pol. rules. L.* 3. c. 22.

Communion, and that they ought to have a Mutual care each of other. *Cant.* 8. 8.

2. The Scripture teacheth that in weighty Cases we should ask Counsel. *2 Sam.* 20. 18. *Prov.* 3. 5. and 15. 22. and 24. 6. Which General Rules concern *Polities* as well as particular Persons, and Churches as well as civil Societies.

3 There are Scripture Examples to instruct us in our Duty herein. We find, that when the Church in *Antioch* had a weighty Case before them, they sent to another Church for Counsel *Act* 15 2 The Apostle *Paul* sought for the Concurrence, and *Right hand of fellowship* of other Apostles *Gala.* 2 9. Ordinary Elders and Churches, have no less need of each other to prevent their *running in vain* *Gal.* 2 2.

4 Such a Communion of Churches as that which we plead for, is no *Innovation*, but that which has ever been the Profession and practice of those that have been called *Congregational* There is a Book which bears the Title of, *An Answer of the Elders of the several Churches in New-England to Thirty two Questions,* Printed in the year 1643. Of which Book my Father *Mather* was the Sole Author. And he wrote it in the Primitive Times of these Churches, (*viz.* in the year 1639) as himself assured me. What he wrote was approved of by other Elders, especially by Mr. *Cotton,* unto whom he Communicated it. Now in Answer to Q 18 *p* 64. are these words, *The Consociation*

G

ation of Churches into Classes and Synods, we hold to be Lawful, and in some cases Necessary: as namely, in things that are not Peculiar to one Church, but Common to them all. And likewise, when a Church is not able to End any matter which concerns only themselves, then they are to seek for Councel and Advice from Neighbour Churches, as the Church at Antioch did send unto the Church at Jerusalem. Act 15. 2 The ground and use of Classes and Synods with the Limitations therein to be Observed, is Summarily laid down by Dr. Ames, unto whom we do wholly Consent in this matter. This was, and is the Judgment of all that adhere to the Order of the Gospel Professed in the Churches of New-England. The world is much mistaken in thinking that Congregational Churches are Independent. That Name has indeed been fastned upon them by their Adversaries ; but our Platform of Discipline Chap. 2. Sect. 5. disclaims the name. And so does our Renowned Hooker (c) in his Survey of Church Discipline. Likewise those famous Apologists in the Assembly at Westminster, viz. Dr. Goodwin, Mr. Nye, Mr. Simpson, Mr. Burrough's, and Mr. Bridge, say that It is a Maxim to be abhorred, that a single and particular Society of men Professing the name of Christ, should Arrogate to themselves an Exemption from giving an account to, or being censurable by Neighbour Churches about them. That Apostle of this Age, (as Dr. Goodwin calls him) Mr. Cotton, the first and forever famous

(c) Part 2. Chap. 3.

famous Teacher in this *Boston*, when he in the Name of the Elders and Messengers of the Churches, gave to Mr. *Mitchel* the right hand of fellowship, at his Ordination to the Pastoral Office in the Church of *Cambridge*, he did in a singular manner recommend to him (and that Excellent man was to his dying day mindful of Mr. *Cottons* Advice) endeavours for the establishment of a *Consociation* amongst the Churches of Christ throughout this *Colony*, that wise man foreseeing that without this, disorder and confusion would in Process of time inevitably happen ; as I have more largely declared in (d) another Discourse in which Mr. *Cottons* proposals respecting the *Consociation* mentioned, are Published to the world, Moreover, that the Concurring Judgment of those who are *Congregational* is according hereunto is Evident from the *Declaration of Faith or Order* which was agreed unto by the Messengers of One hundred and Twenty Congregational Churches in *England*, who met at the *Savoy* in *London*, Anno 1658 They thus declare, (e) *In case of difficulties and differances in point of Doctrine, wherein either the Churches in general are concerned in their peace, union, and edification, or any Member or Members of any Church are injured in, or by any proceeding in Censures not agreeable to Truth and Order : It is according to the mind of Christ, that many Churches holding Communion together,*

G 2

do

(d) *In my first Principles of N. E. p 28. &c.*

do by their Meſſengers meet in a Synod or Council, to Conſider and give their Advice in, or about the matter in differance. But the Teſtimony of that Bleſſed *Jeremiah Burrough* puts the thing beyond all diſpute. For his words are theſe (f) *Thoſe in the Congregational way acknowledge.*

1. *That they are bound in Conſcience to give account: of their wayes to Churches about them, or to any other who ſhall require it. This not in an Arbitrary way, but as a duty which they owe to God and Man.*

2. *They acknowledge that Synods of other Miniſters and Elders about them are an Ordinance of Jeſus Chriſt for the helping the Church againſt Errors, Schiſms and Scandals.*

3. *That theſe Synods may from the power they have from Chriſt, admoniſh men and Churches in his Name, when they ſee evils continuing in, or growing upon the Church, and their admonitions carry with them the Authority of Jeſus Chriſt.*

4. *As there ſhall be cauſe, they may declare men or Churches to be ſubverters of the Faith, or otherwiſe according to the nature of their offence, to ſhame them before all the Churches about them.*

5. *They may by a ſolemn act in the Name of Jeſus Chriſt, refuſe any further Communion with them till they repent.*

6. *They may declare alſo in the Name of Chriſt, that thoſe erring People or Churches are not to be received into fellowſhip with any of the*

(f) *In his Irenicum p* 43, 44, 47.

*the Churches of Christ, nor to have Commu-
nion with any other in the Ordinances of Christ*

If it shall be said, surely they do not come
up to these six things mentioned. To that I
Answer (says Mr. *Burroughs*) *I do not in these
deliver only my own Judgment, but by what I
know of the Judgment of all those Brethren with
whom I have occasion to converse by Conferance
both before and since, I stand charged to make
it good to be their Judgment also ; yea, it has
been theirs and mine for divers years, even then
when we never thought to have enjoyed our
own Land again.* We see by these *Testimonies*
that *Congregational men* in general, as well as
the *Churches of New England* in special, are no
such *Independents,* no such *Brownists,* no such
Morellians, as some have represented them to
be.

5. If we admit not a *Consociation of Churches,*
there will be no Remedy against the *Male-
Administrations* of Particular Churches ; nor
any cure of Schisms, or Errors that may happen
in our Churches. This has been objected
(but injuriously) as a Scandal attending *the
Congregational Church discipline,* and that
therefore it is *a way not practicable.* Indeed,
if we refuse this part of *Church Communion,* the
objection would be unanswerable. And who
would be willing to be a Member of that
Church, in which although he should be never
so much wronged, there will be no relief for
him upon Earth ? There was once a Church
in *New-England,* which having censured one of
their

G 3

their Members, he complained of the supposed wrong done him, to Neighbour Elders, who thought he had received hard measure. The Pastor and major part of the Church were not willing the case should have a re-hearing before the Elders and Messengers of other Churches. Upon this, great clamours were raised, and prejudices taken up against the Congregational Discipline. Mr. *Cawdrey* got this story by the end, and in his *Epistle to the Dissenting Brethren p.* 10. He sayes that a Minister in *N E.* writes over to *England,* that this injured person would have *no remedy until the Churches in New-England were become Presbyterians, and that if Independency does not break all the Churches in New-England excepting a few Semi-Presbyterian, some are deceived* Who the Minister was that wrote thus to *England,* Mr. *Cawdrey* tells us not. But it is a great wrong to the Churches of *New-England,* and to the *way Congregational,* to Represent them, and all that are of *that way,* as being of such *Independent and Unaccountable Principles,* which they utterly disclaim. Dr. *Owen* in his *Disciplinary Catechism,* and especially in the *Additament there unto,* (which was written on occasion of an harsh and rash censure in the *Independent Church in Cambridge* in *England*) has with great evidence of reason, refuted the maintainers of such an *Independency.*

6. The order asserted is (as has been truly observed by the Learned *Doctor* last mentioned) confirmed by the practice of the first Churches

after

after the Apostles : for when the Church in
Corinth had by an undue Exercise of Discipline
deposed some of their Elders, the Church of
Rome taking Cognizance of it, wrote to them,
reproving their rashness, and advised their restoration, as it is to be seen in the Epistle of
Clement than Pastor of the Church in *Rome*,
which *Clement* is thought to be the same whom
Paul speaks of, *Phil.* 4. 3. And when the
Church of *Antioch* was afterwards troubled
with the Heresies of their Pastor *Samosetanus*,
the Neighbouring Pastors came unto the
Church, and joyned their concurrence in his
deposition. It is certain that in the next Ages
to the Apostles, a Pastor was not settled in any
Church without the Concurrence of others.
When the Church had Elected a Pastor, they
presented him to the Neighbour Pastors for
their Approbation, nor could he be legally
confirmed without it. (g) *Eusebius* tells us that
when *Alexander* was chosen Pastor of the
Church in *Jerusalem* by the Brethren of that
place, he had the common consent of the
Circumjacent Pastors. And thus (as *Cyprian*
informs us) it was practised in all the
Churches throughout *Africa.* He speaks particularly concerning *Sabinus*, who was Elected
a Pastor of *Eremita* in *Spain*, that Neighbour
Ministers concured in his Ordination, after the
Fraternity had Elected him. His words are (h)

Quod

(g) *Lib.* 5. *c* 11
(h) *Cyprian Epist.* 68.

Quod factum videmus in sabini Ordinatione ut de universæ fraternitatis suffragio, & de Episcoporum judicio, Episcopatus ei deferetur. We find in *Ecclesiastical Story*, that in the Primitive Times the Names of Persons to be Ordained were Published abroad that so if any one had ought to object they might produce it. Which custom of the Christians in the Election of their Pastors was so highly approved of by the Emperor *Severus*, as that he would have it put in practice in Establishing Governours of Provinces throughout the Empire.

7. Neither do the Reformed Churches Ordain a Minister without the concurrence and approbation of Neighbour Ministers. To *give the Right hand of Fellowship* to a new Ordained Minister, was a usual custom amongst the Churches in *Bohemia*, for which they alledged that Scripture, *Gal.* 2. 9. as is Testifyed by (*i*) *Commenius*. In the beginning of the *Reformation* in the Church of *Scotland*, one Article of their discipline, is, That *when a Minister is Ordained the rest of the Ministers shall take the Elected by the hand in sign of their consent*, as is related in the *History of the Reformation* (*k*) which goeth under the Name of Mr. *Knox*. I find also, that there is the like practice in the Protestant *French Churches*. When a Minister is Ordained, two Deputies of the *Synod* or *Colloque* are appointed *in the presence of the People, to give him the Right-hand*

(i) *Rat. ordin discipl* p. 33.
(k) *Page* 285.

hand of Fellowship. These things I have the rather mentioned for the Information of our young Divines, who being Unstudied in the Controversies of Church discipline, are apt to think that the custom of giving *the Right hand of Fellowship at Ordinations,* is a *Novelty* and *Singularity* practised no where but in *New-England,* whenas it was used in other Churches long before there was a *New-England* in the world. But (not to divert) the *French Protestant Discipline* will by no means allow that a Minister should intrude himself into any Church, without the approbation of Neighbour Pastors. One of the Articles of their Discipline is in these words, *The Minister that shall intrude himself, although he were approved by the People, is not to be approved by Neighbour Ministers or others.* A late (l) Author that Comments on this Article of the *French discipline,* observes that it holds a Conformity with the practice of the Churches in the primitive Times. For the Council of *Antioch* has this Canon, *If a Bishop out of Employment intrude himself into a Vacant Church, and usurp the place without the Authority of a Synod, Let him be turned out, although he may be approved by all the People, which he shall have gained to him.* Thus careful have Churches been, both in former and in later ages that in the Establishment of a Minister, the concurrence Neighbour Elders should be endeavoured.

And

(l) *La. Roque p.* 23.

And this which has been said is consonant to the Articles agreed unto by the *United Brethren* at *London* They declare, *That in so weighty a matter as calling and chusing a Pastor, we Judge it ordinarily requisite, that every such Church consult and advise with the Pastors of Neighbouring Congregations.* And that, *It is Ordinarily requisite that the Pastors of Neighbouring Congregations concur in the Ordination of the Person chosen by the Brother-hood of that Particular Church.* That word *Ordinarily* is well put in, because in a Time of Persecution that cannot be done, which in a Time of Liberty may, and ought to be attended. The Presbyterian discipline of *France*, requires that a Minister shall not be admitted to his Office, but by the Provincial Synod ; *except* (say they) *it be in troublesome Times,* and then he may be ordained with the Approbation of only three Ministers. The like to which was decreed in the *Synod* of *Nice*, that ordinarily all the Pastors of a Province should concur in the Ordination of a Pastor, but in case of an urgent necessity so requiring, it might be done with the concurrence of three Pastors. And these things may serve to justify a former Law made by the civil Government in this *Colony*, That *no person should be Ordained a Minister in any Church*, but with the Approbation of the Elders and Messengers of four Neighbouring Churches. This practice although it has not at present

the

the Authority of the civil Law to confirm
it, nevertheless, being grounded upon Scripture and right reason, it ought to be Sacred
unto us.

QUESTION. XI.

MAY the Brethren in Churches and not the
Pastors only be sent unto, and have
their Voice in Ecclesiastical Councils?

Answ. We maintain the *Affirmative* in this
Question. In the last General *Synod* which
was in *New-England*, viz. That which met at
Boston in the year 1679. Some Churches sent
only their *Elders* without any *Brethren*:
which the *Synod* was so far unsatisfied with,
as that they would not allow those *Pastors*
to sit with them, until they had prevailed
with their Churches to send *Brethren* also,
being very tender of admitting any thing
that should look like an infringement of that
Liberty and priviledge which does by the
Institution of Christ belong to the *Brother-
hood* in particular Churches. The reasons of
our Judgement are such as these.

1. The first Synod that ever was in which
a Copy and Sampler is left to all Succeeding
Generations, did consist not only of *Elders*
but of *Brethren*, who had their voice therein, namely the Synod at *Jerusalem*, of which
Act.

Act. 15. giveth us the account. The 4th. verse speaketh of *the Church* as well as of the *Apostles and. Elders.* Now he that was in his Time *the Oracle of the University of Cambridge* argueth thus, (*m*) why was the cause brought *to the People* and not to the *Elders only*, if they had not power to judge in the case? And he therefore concludes against *Bellarmine*, that every *Laice* in that *Synod* had a difinitive suffrage as much as *Peter* himself. And whereas *Bellarmine* objects, that *the Brethren did only hear and not speak*, in that Assembly *Whitaker* argues from verse 12 That *the Brethren had been (not tumultuously but in an orderly manner) declaring their apprehensions on the case under controversy*; or however that the Expression in that *Verse* implys, that they had a Liberty of Speech granted to them. And in verse 22. 'tis said, *It pleased* the Apostles and Elders *with the whole Church, &c.* In the Council of *Basil*, it was argued, that that word, *It pleased*, being spoken not of the Elders only, but of others, it does Evidently import, that those other, even *the Members of the Church* had also a power of Judgment and determination in the Question then under debate. From thence likewise does *Juel* against *Harding* prove that *Laicks* (as they calls the *Brethren* in Churches) have this power of right belonging to them, to *Sit and Judge in Ecclesiastical Councils.* And so does Dr. *Wills*

the Authority of the civil Law to confirm
it, neverthelefs, being grounded upon Scripture and right reafon, it ought to be Sacred
unto us.

QUESTION. XI.

MAY the Brethren in Churches and not the
Paftors only be fent unto, and have
their Voice in Ecclefiaftical Councils?

Anwf. We maintain the *Affirmative* in this
Queftion In the laft General *Synod* which
was in *New-England*, viz. That which met at
Bofton in the year 1679. Some Churches fent
only their *Elders* without any *Brethren:*
which the *Synod* was fo far unfatisfyed with,
as that they would not allow thofe *Paftors*
to fit with them, until they had prevailed
with their Churches to fend *Brethren* alfo,
being very tender of admitting any thing
that fhould look like an infringement of that
Liberty and priviledge which does by the
Inftitution of Chrift belong to the *Brother-
hood* in particular Churches. The reafons of
our Judgement are fuch as thefe.

1. The firft Synod that ever was in which
a Copy and Sampler is left to all Succeeding
Generations, did confift not only of *Elders*
but of *Brethren,* who had their voice therein, namely the Synod at Jerufalem, of which
Act.

Act. 15. giveth us the account. The 4*th.* verse speaketh of *the Church* as well as of the *Apostles and. Elders.* Now he that was in his Time *the Oracle of the University of Cambridge* argueth thus, (*m*) why was the cause brought *to the People* and not to the *Elders only*, if they had not power to judge in the case? And he therefore concludes against *Bellarmine*, that every *Laice* in that *Synod* had a disinitive suffrage as much as *Peter* himself. And whereas *Bellarmine* objects, that *the Brethren did only hear and not speak,* in that Assembly *Whitaker* argues from verse 12 That *the Brethren had been (not tumultueusly but in an orderly manner) declaring their apprehensions on the case under controversy ;* or however that the Expression in that *Verse* implys, that they had a Liberty of Speech granted to them. And in verse 22. 'tis said, *It pleased* the Apostles and Elders *with the whole Church, &c.* In the Council of *Basil*, it was argued, that that word, *It pleased,* being spoken not of the Elders only, but of others, it does Evidently import, that those other, even *the Members of the Church* had also a power of Judgment and determination in the Question then under debate. From thence likewise does *Juel* against *Harding* prove that *Laicks* (as they calls the *Brethren* in Churches) have this power of right belonging to them, to *Sit and Judge in Ecclesiastical Councils.* And so does Dr. *Wise*

(m) *Whitaker de Conciliis.*

Willet (n) (a Learned and worthy Conforma-
ble Divine of the Church of *England*) from
that same Scripture conclude. Moreover, in
in *Verf.* 23. 'tis said, that the Letters containing
the *Decrees* of that *Council* were Sent (and
consequently signed) in the Name *of the Brethren* as well as of the Apostles and Elders.
Which shows that they had some-thing else to
do in that *Synod* than only to keep silence,
and hear what others had to say. Wherefore
Dr. *Owen* might well say, (o) That *in Synods,
It is not necessary that Elders alone should be sent
by the Churches, but they may have others joyned
with them, and had so until* prelatical usurpa-
*tion over-turned their Liberty. There were ma-
ny besides* Paul *and* Barnabas *sent from* Antioch
to Jerusalem, *and the* Brethren *of that Church,
whatever is impudently pretended to the contrary,
concurred in the decree and determination there
made.* Thus. Dr. *Owen.*

2. There is weight in *Austins* Argument,
viz. That the power of the Keyes belongs to
the whole Church : And that therefore not the
Pastors only should have their voice in Councils. Since Councils represent the Churches
by whom they are chosen, it is meet that
some of each order should be chosen. Church-
Members are fellow Citizens, and therefore
ought not to be deprived of their power.

H   3. It

(n) *In Synops papism. Cont* 3 Q. 3 *p.* 125.
(o) *Of a G spel Church.* p 263.

3. It is not their Office but the Churches *Delegation* that giveth power to be the Members in *Synods*. The *Specificating act* in which *Synodal power* and so the right of a *Decisive Vote* is founded, is the Churches *Delegation*. None ought to be Admitted into such Assemblies, but those whom the Churches shall send. Now as in Civil Councils, many times not only Magestrates but other Citizens duely qualified are sent to represent the City whose delegates they are; so in *Ecclesiastical Councils*, not only the Rulers of the Churches, but others may receive a mission from them, and have then and there, equal power with the former. True it is, that of these *Delegates* from the Churches, the *Elders* ought to be the principally concerned. They are presumed best to know the state of their Churches, and to be best able to Judge in *Ecclesiastical Affairs*. This notwithstanding, they are not to assume the sole power to themselves, nor yet a Negative Voice in in such Assemblies, as they may in their own particular Churches. It must (sayes Dr *Owen*) (p) *be affirmed that no persons by Vertue of any Office meerly, have right to be Members of Ecclesiastical Synods as such. Neither is there either example or reason to give colour to any such pretence. Officers of the Church, Bishops, Pastors, Elders, may be present in them, ought to be present in them, are meetest for the most part so to be, but* meerly as such, *it belongs not unto them.* This will seem to some to be *Independant*

(p) *Ibid. p* 260.

pendent Doctrine. But that is their mistake.
Bullinger,, Hyperius, Danæus, Voetius, and a
mongst our English writers *Whitaker, Parker*
and other great Divines have affirmed as much
as this comes to   Yea, the generality of our
Divines in their disputations against the Papists
Episcopal Monopoly of *Synodal Power,* reason as
we do.   And it is clear from this Argument.
If it belongs to Elders *as such* to be Members
of *Synods,* then *all such* must be there.   But if
so, then in case a *Synod* should continue sitting
a year together (as it often happens) all that
while the Particular Churches to whom those
Elders belong that are remote from the place
where the *Synod* meets, must not have one
Eder to instruct and guide them.

4 The Questions which are handled and
decided in *Synods* are commonly such as *Brethren*
and not Elders only are concerned in.   This
Reason is urged by our *Juel* (a great light in
the English Church) in his defence of the
Church of England.   Yea, some Learned Papists
have been so ingenuous as to confess there is
weight in it.   *That which pertains to all is not
valid, if some of all sorts have not a consent in
it ;* which assertion (sayes Dr *Field* writing
against the *Romanists*) ha's its foundation in
nature and in reason.

5 In some Churches there are Brethren
whose gifts and abilities are beyond their Pastors.
And why should not such be Members of
Ecclesiastical Councils, and have a suffrage
therein equal with any others ?   In some

Monasteries of old there were Readers of Divinity, whose work it was (as the incomparable (q) *Usher* has observed) to instruct *Clergy men:* There are at this day in some *Universities,* Learned professors of *Theology* (who are not Pastors of any Church) perhaps more able to give light in a difficult Controversy than any *Elder* in the *Synod* What reason can be given why Churches should not delegate such, or why they should not have *decisive Votes* as well as any others ?

6. The most Famous *Synods* which have been in the world have consisted not of Elders only. That in the next Ages to the Apostles others besides Pastors were Members of *Ecclesiastical Councils,* our Divines in their writings against the Papists have proved. In the Council of *Calcedon* there were Seven Earles, and ten noble Senators, and not *Ecclesiasticks* only. Since the Reformation, the Churches of *Sweveland* (r) Petitioned that there might be a *Council* called *of every degree and state* consisting of the best Learned and most Godly men whom the Province did afford. In the famous *Synod* of *Dort,* there were besides Pastors, Professors of Divinity, and many *Seniors* or *Ruling Elders* who were not ordained Officers. In the *Assembly* at *Westminster* which met *July* 1. 1643. There were not only Pastors of Churches, but several noble men,

e. g.

(q) *de Success Eccles. c. 7. s. 24.*
(r) *See Harmon. of Confessions. p. 602.*

e. g. The Earl of *Pembrooke*, the Lord *Say*, the Lord *Wharton* (who told me Eight years agoe, that he was the only person of that Affembly then living) and several others of the Nobility, and some Gentlemen of the House of Commons, Mr. *Selden*, Mr. *Rouse*, Mr. *Whitlock* and others : Also Commiffioners from *Scotland* were joyned with them, *e. g.* The Earl of *Lothian*, Lord *Warriftone*, Lord *Lauderdale*, befides Minifters from that Kingdom. So then it is not an *Independent Phanfy*, that Affemblies met to confult about Ecclefiaftical and Religious Controverfies fhould confift of other Perfons befides Ecclefiafticks.

7. Some not found in the Faith have thought it their intereft to maintain the Negative in this Queftion In an old Heretical Council (s) there was an out-cry, *Synodus Epifcoporum eft*, Synods fhould confift of none but Bifhops, others are Superfluous. So do the Papifts Teach: They fay that in the Synod *Act* 15. only the Apoftles were Judges, and that the *Laics*, or *Brethren there had nothing to do but to hear and fubmit their Judgments and Confent to what the other fhould determine.* Juft after the fame manner do fome *Prelate Proteftants*, particularly *Sutlift*, and *Bridges* exprefs themfelves. The Jefuit *Sanders* railes againft the *Magdeburgenfes* becaufe in their *Eccl fiaftical Hiftory* they affirm that *Laicks* were Members of Synods. N ne (fayes he) but

H 3

but

(s) V. *Willet ubi fupra.* p. 127.

but mad-men can believe that Mechanicks should
sit in Council with Bishops to Judge of Ecclesiastical affairs. But as to that objection, that
Illiterate persons are not fit to be in Synods
there to determine Questions wherein Religion
is concerned, a very Learned *Dutch* (t) Divine
giveth a double Answer.

1. That some who are not Pastors of
Churches are nevertheless men of great Learn-
ing as were many of the *Seniors* in the Synod of
Dort.

2. That some who do not excel in Scholasti-
cal Learning are versed in the Holy Scriptures,
and in Zeal and Piety Excel some Ministers.
Many *Seniors* with us (sayes he) abode by the
Truth, when their Pastors did not so, in the
Time when the *Arminian Remonstrants* made
a disturbance in the Churches.

(t) *Voet pol. Eccles part* 3. *p* 195.

QUESTION. XII.

DOES the Essence of a Ministers Call Consist
in his being Ordained with the Imposition
of hands by other Ministers ?

Answ. There are who say that it does
And that the Minister imposing hands must be
a Bishop, or otherwise it is no valid Ordination
Which notion makes all (or most of) the
Minister

Ministers in *France*, *Switzerland*, *Denmark*, *Holland*, *Scotland* &c. to be no true Ministers for want of *Episcopal Ordination*. We have these things to offer to the contrary.

1. The Essence of a Ministers Call consists in a mutual Election between him and his People. As in Marriage the Consent of both parties is Essentially requisite, but a publick Solemnization of the Marriage is not so. The *Coronation* of a King is not Essential to his Office, nor is the Solemn *Inauguration* of a Publick Magistrate Essential to his being a Magistrate. No more is *Ordination* to the being of a Minister Learned Papists notwithstanding they are wont to place the Essence of a Ministers Call in his Ordination, says that a *Cardinal* has his Ecclesiastical power by vertue of his *Election* before his *Installment* And that a *Pope* when Elected has Power to rule the Church before his *Inthronization*. The Lawyers say that *Solennia non sunt de rei Substantia*. We cannot say that if a man has not received Imposition of hands that then he is no Pastor, but we may say that if he has not been Elected by some Church of Christ he is no Pastor, but his Ordination is a nullity. For which cause the Learned (*u*) and noble *Morney* approves of *Chrysostom*, his saying that *Election by the People is so necessary that without it there is neither Altar, nor Priesthood*. And a whole Council, viz. that of *Calcedon* has pronounced

(u) *Of the Church.* Cha. 11. p. 129.

nounced all such *Ordinations* to be null, as we shall afterwards have occasion more fully to declare. Suppose a person qualified with Ministerial gifts should suffer Shipwrack in a remote Island where there are none but Heathen, and should by Preaching be instrumental in the Conversion of many of them, might not these his Converts Elect him to be their Pastor, and might not he accepting of their Call, Administer all Ordinances to them without any Ordination by the Imposition of the hands of Ministers, where there are no Ministers? Mr. *Herle* a Learned Presbyterian does not deny it. And Dr. *Whitaker* (w) affirms no less in saying, that *if there were not a Bishop in the World the Church could Create Bishops* Ecclesiastical Story informs us, That *Ædisius* and *Frumentus* being private men by Preaching the Gospel Converted a great Nation of Indians, Might they not Administer Sacraments to these Converts being Elected by them to be their Pastor, without any Imposition of hands from other Pastors in a Country where none were. See Dr. *Fulk* on *Rom.* 10 15.

2. Not only *Congregational Men*, but many of the *Presbyterian Judgment*, and others also, esteem the *Imposition of Hands* to be an indifferent and not a necessary thing. That which may be either done or left undone without Sin. Thus do the Presbyterians in *Scotland* declare. In the *History of the Church of*

(w) *de pen. tis. Roman Quest. I. cap. 1. §. p 300.*

of Scotland written by Mr. *Calderwood,* p. 26.
It is afferted that *Impofition of hands they judge not necefary in the Admiffion of Minifters* And when in the year 1597. that *Queftion* was by the King put to the General Affembly (x) *Is he a Lawful Paftor who wants Impofition of hands?* Their Anfwer was in thefe words, *Impofition or Laying on of hands is not Effential and necefare, but Ceremonial and indifferent in the Admiffion of a Paftor.* This does Mr. *Gilefpy* alfo maintain in his Learned *Difcourfe againft Englifh Popifh Ceremonies* p 285 The Dutch Churches efteem Impofion of hands to be *Adiaphorous.* And therefore fomtimes in the Ordination of Paftors they omit that Ceremony ; and they never ufe it in the *Ordination* either of *Ruling Elders* or of *Deacons.* So far as I can learn, the Churches of *New England* are the only ones in the World that Ordain Ruling Elders or Deacons with the Impofition of hands. (y) *Pifcator, Daneus, Alting Zepperus, Polanus,* declare it to be *Indifferent.* So do *Biduinus, Gerhard* and other writers (of the *Lutheran* perfwafion. In fome places in (z) *Germany* they ufe this *Rite of Impofing hands,* in the Ordination of Minifters, in Baptifm, and in Confirmaion, and at Marriage alfo, but in all as a tning *Adiaphorous.*

3. If

(x) *Calderwood Hift of Church of Scotl* p. 382.
(y) In 1 Tim 4. 14 —
(z) V. *Voet de pol. Ecclef.* part 1. L. 2.
p. 465.

3. If we make the Essence of a Minister,
Call, to consist in his Ordination by imposition
of hands from other Lawful Ministers, it will
be a difficult thing to prove that our first *Reformers* were true Ministers of Christ. As for
Ordination in the Church of *Rome* some of
them renounced it, not at all supposing
themselves to be Ministers of Christ meerly on
that account.   They thought it was their
duty, *inordinatissimam Ordinationem ejurare*,
as *Beza* speaks. Some of them never had it.
For they did first Preach without any formal
Call or Allowance of those who usurped the
Title of Pastors and Bishops, and the Sole
power of Ordination, and were afterwards
called to the Ministry by the Churches which
they had taught. *Tilenus* being demanded
of the *Earl of Laval* from whom *Calvin* had his
Calling, Answered, from the Church of *Geneva*, and from *Farel* his Predecessor, who had
also his from the People of *Geneva*, who had
Right and Authority to institute and depose
Ministers. *Bellarmine* objects that the Protestants have no true Ministers among them,
because they have not received Ordination by
Imposition of hands *Successively* from the Apostles. Dr. *Willet* in Answer thereto sayes,
(a) *In the Corrupt times of the Gospel the Lord
has raised up Faithful Ministers to his Church
that could shew no Succession from the Degenerate
Clergy.* They that stand upon a Lineal Succession

(a) *Synopsis Contr* 2. Q 13. *p.* 81.

cession of Ordination from the Apostles, must
of necessity own the Church of *Rome* to be
a true Church, and (the *Bishops* of *Rome*) *the
Ministers of Antichrist* to be the true Ministers
of Christ. For Churches to go to them for
Ordained Ministers, is (sayes *Melanchon*) as
if the Sheep should go to Wolves for She-
pherds. It has been well said by those who
have gone before us, That *God does so much
abhor Antichrist that he would not have his People to seek to him, nor to his Priests to Ordain
Christs Ministers, as he would not take of Baby-
lon a Stone for a corner, nor a Stone for a
Foundation.* Jer. 51. 16 Whereas *it is objected
(sayes* Mr. *Perkins) That they who are Lawfully called are Ordained by them whose Aun-
cesters have been Successively Ordained by the A-
postles. I Answer, there is a Succession of Doctrine
in which our Ministers Succeed the Apostles, and
this is sufficient. If in Turkey, or America, or
else where the Gospel should be received by the
Counsil and parswasion of private Persons, they
shall not need to send to Europe for Consecrated
Ministers, but they have power to Chuse their own
Ministers from within themselves.* Thus Mr.
Perkins To the like purpose does (†) *Zanchy*
speak. And *Voetius* in his Learned Book concerning the *Desperate cause of Papacy,* has made
it as clear as the Light of the Sun, that not
a *Personal Succession,* but a Succession in respect
of

(b) On *Gala.* 2 11.
(†) In *Eph.* 5. *ubi de Baptismo.*

of Doctrine is neceſſary to make a true Miniſter of Chriſt.

4. There are Judicious and Learned men who conceive that others beſides Miniſters may Impoſe hands in the Ordination of Miniſters. This is aſſerted *in our Platform of Diſcipline,* which had the Approbation of many Divines as Eminent for Piety and Learning as moſt which this Age has produced. Nor is this which will ſeem a very ſtrange *Aſſertion* to ſome, a notion peculiar to *New-England Divines* only. Others of as deep Judgment as any whom the World has known, have maintained the ſame. Dr. *Ames* (c) ſayes, that as the power of Seeing is formally and ſubjectively in the Eye, yet originally in the whole Animal, ſo is the power of Ordination in the whole Church, and that therefore although in a well conſtituted Church, the Act of Ordination is to be performed by the Elders, *in caſe duely qualifyed Elders are not to be had, Ordination may be performed by non Elders.* And that in a Corrupt ſtate of the Church where Order and Miniſtry fails, *A plebe actus Ordinationis Legitime fieri poteſt,* the People may Ordain. Dr. *Whitaker* (d) affirms, that they that have power to Call have power to Ordain. And that *the Church has power both to Call a Biſhop and to Ordain him alſo.* Not only Congregational men, but ſome *Presbyterians* whoſe

(c) *Bellerm enervat Tom. 2. L 3 cap 2.*
(d) *De pontifice. Rom. Q 2. c. 15.*
et de Eccleſia. Q 5 c. 6.

whose great Learning and Piety has made them Eminent, have said as much as is in our *Platform of Discipline* affirmed concerning *Ordination.* *Voetius* (a) asserts, *That the Church may delegate a Member of their body to Ordain a* Presbyter, *or may wholly omit the Solemnity of a Consecration, and that the Person chosen to the Ministry, may by vertue of his Election perform the acts belonging to his Ministerial Office.* The very same is affirmed by *Dideclavius.* p. 242. And by Mr. *Gillespy* against the Ceremonies. p. 286. Also *Gerson Bucer* (†) maintains that in case the *Eldership* should wholly fail the power of Ordination remains with the Church. The Defenders of this *Problem* alledge such Reasons for it, as deserve Consideration. *e. g.*

1 That we read in the Scriptures of *Non-Officers imposing their hands* upon such as were set apart unto a Sacred Office. The *Levites* were *Ecclesiastical Officers,* but the Children of Israel who imposed hands on them were not so *Numb* 8. 10.

2 We read in *the New-Testament* of *Ordinary Officers imposing hands* on them who were *Extraordinary* Officers. Thus *Ananias* imposed hands on *Paul, Act.* 9 And after that, the Elders of the Church in *Antioch* imposed hands on *Paul and Barnabas. Act.* 13. 3. And not only *Paul* but the Elders of the Church in *Ephesus* imposed hands on *Timothy,* who was an *Evange-*
list

i

(a) *Desp cam. pap. L.* 2 *c.* 2. *p.* 269, 274.
(†) *De Guber. Ecclef. p.* 262, 263.

ist and therefore an Extraordinary Officer.
Now if an ordinary Officer may lay his hands
on one that is Extraordinary, why may not a
Non-Elder appointed thereunto by the Church,
do the like to one that is only an Ordinary Presbyter? This clearly Answers what *Papists* and
Prelates are wont to object, *viz.* that the
Ordainer is greater than the Ordained, and
that therefore none but *Bishops* ought to Ordain or impose hands, as being a degree above
Presbyters. But was *Ananias* greater then the
Apostle *Paul*? or the Ministers in the Church
of *Antioch* greater then *Paul and Barnabas*?
or the Presbyters in *Ephesus* greater then *Timothy*? In the beginning of the *Reformation* in
England several who had never been Ordained
Priests by *Bishops*, were nevertheless made Bishops, as is observed in the late *Collection of Sta*
Tracts. p. 50. Some *Councils* have allowed of
the Ordination of *Bishops* in a case of necessity
when *Bishops* were not at hand, by those who
were no *Bishops*, but inferiour to them, which
neither do some of our Episcopal Writers gain-
say: And notwithstanding the *Council of Tren*
has declared all *Secular Ordinations* to be
nullities, that dos not make them to be so.

3. *Imposition of hands* in Ordination is not
a *Sacrament* (as many of our Divines have
proved against the Papists) nor has it any
Religious Significancy in it. No doubt but the
Rite might Lawfully be used at the *Inaugura*
tion of some *Civil Officers*, as the Jews from
whom it is borrowed, *Imposed hands* on a S-

nati

ator when Solemnly admitted into the great
Sanedrin, and upon a *Doctor* in one of their
Colledges when admitted to a *Rabbinatus* as
Alting (*e*) shows : Though sometimes they
were *Promoted* without any Imposition of hands
as *Buxtorfe* (*f*) out of the Jewish Writers inform us

4. Mr *Hookers* Judgment, is, that *Ordination* is not an act of *Authority* but of *Order*
only. And that therefore it may be performed by Non-Officers. As for that Objection
which some have thought weighty. *viz.* *That
none can give what himself has not*, and that
therefore men upon whom hands were never
imposed cannot impose hands upon others,
it is easily Answered, men may give that which
they are not formally only vertually the Subjects of A Nation by chusing a King, give him
Legal Power.   A City by Chusing a Lord
Mayor, make him a Magistrate.   A Woman
by giving her self in Marriage causeth the man
to whom she giveth her self to have the
Power of an Husband : but no man will be
so absurd as to say, that a Woman has formally the power of an Husband   In former
Ages the Kings of *England* in their *Charters* to
Abbats and *Bishops* (†) gave them power to
Ordain Monks and Clerks : But those Kings
I 2   were

(*e*) *De Academia Hebr.*
(*f*) *Lexic. Thalmud.* p. 1498.
(†) *v. Malmesbury de Gest: Reg.
Angl. L.* 2. *c* 7, 8.

were not themselves Ecclesiastical Officers, or *Ordained* Notwithstanding all this Discourse, I am far from approving that which ha's been practised in some Churches, who when Neighbour Elders were present, have improved Brethren to impose hands on their Pastors. I think it were better to have an *Ordination* with Fasting and Prayer only, without any imposition of hands, (as is practised in many Congregations in *England*) then to have that unnecessary Ceremony performed by *Non-Elders*. The Old Doctrine of *New England*, was, *That if the Church where Ordination is to be performed has not Elders of its own, they shou'd desire Neighbour Elders to Assist in the Ordination of their Pastor, and that with Imposition of hands as well as with Fasting and Prayer.* Most true it is, that we read not in the New-Testament of the Imposition of hands by Non-Elders, because then Elders were not wanting to perform that Service and to make use of *Non Elders* in this affair when Elders might be obtained is not decent, nor approved of by those great Divines that do not absolutely deny the Lawfulness of such a practice. I shall only add, that *Daneus*, in his *Commentary* on 1 Tim. 5 22. *p.* 361. does not only maintain that imposition of hands is not a necessary Ceremony in the Constitution of a Minister; but sayes, that it is *Fatuity* to do as the Papists do, in making the *Essence* of a Legitimate vocation to the Ministry, to consist therein, and that to make it a Question, *whether the same person may receive*

ceive imposition of hands more than once ; is to
propose *a vain and inept Question*, because it
is not material whether it be ever done at all.

QUESTION XIII.

MAY *a man be Ordained a Pastor, Except
to a particular Church, and in the presence of that Church?*

Answ There are two parts of this *Question*,
which we shall Answer distinctly.

1. We assert that no man ought to be Ordained a Pastor, Except unto a particular,
Church. For,

1. We have no Instance in the Scripture of
ordinary Officers Ordained, Except unto a
particular Flock. *Act* 14 23. *They Ordained
Elders by Election* (so does the *Geneva* Translation read the words truly enough as that Learned Knight, Sir *Norton Knatchbull* (†) has criti-
cally evinced) *in every Church. Paul* left it
in Charge with *Titus*, that he should *Ordain
Elders in every City. Tit.* 1. 5. He was not to
Ordain them to be *Individua vaga*, but a particular place, a City wherein was some Church
was assigned to them to Labour in. He might
not (as Mr. *Baynes* and from him (g) *Didocla-
I 3   vit*

(†) *In Animadv. in Libr. N. T.*
(g) *Altare Damascen. p. 209.*

view speaks.) Ordain Elders as the University Creates *Doctors of Physick,* without assigning them any Patients, or as they make *Masters of Art* without providing for them any Scholars.

2. Pastor and Flock are Relates, and therefore one cannot be without the other. It is contrary to the Rules of Reason (as Logicians know) that the *Relate* should be without its *Correlate.* (h) To say that a *Wandring Levite* who has no Flock is a Pastor, is as good sense as to say, that he that has no Children is a Father, and that the man who has no Wife is a Husband Nor may it be pretended that the *Catholick Church* is his Flock. For (not to insist on the common Protestant Doctrine that the *Catholick Church is Invisible* ; as comprehending all true Believers from *Abel* to the End of the World)

3. A Pastor is under an Obligation to feed every one that is of the Flock which he is a Pastor unto. Act. 20 28 *Take heed therefore to your selves, and to all the Flock over which the Holy Ghost has made you Overseers* Is any meer man able to feed *all that Flock* of the Church Catholick Visible ? A Minister must give an account concerning every Soul in that Flock which he is the Pastor of. *Heb.* 13 17 They that say they are *Pastors of the Catholick Church,* may do well to think what account they can give of the ten thousands of Souls belonging to
their

(h) *Voet de d sper. causa papa-*
tus. p. 238.

their Flock that were never instructed nor fed by them.

4 Supposing a man to have a Particular Church to which he is related, if he is a Pastor to other Churches besides that, then it is not in the power of that Church to deprive him of his Pastoral Office. If they should reject him and that deservedly from being their Pastor, he may pretend, I am a Pastor of the Catholick Church, and will be so, do you do your worst. This savours of the Papists *indelible Character*, who pretend that if a man has been once *Ordained*, he can never be a *Laic* again. Then a person who is justly not only deposed from his Office, but Excommunicated, may be a Pastor still. And if so, then he that is not so much as a Member of the Visible Church may yet be a *Pastor of the Church Catholick*, for one justly Excommunicate, is no longer of Christ's Visible Kingdom, being Authoritatively declared to belong unto Satan. Our *Discipline* declares not only that such as never were related to a particular Flock, but such as have been, but now are not so related, to be no Church Officers. The words in the *Platform*, Ch 9 S. 7 Are, *He that is clearly loosed from his Office-relation unto that Church whereof he was a Minister, cannot be look'd at as an Officer, nor perform any act of Office in any other Church, unless he be again orderly called unto Office.*

5. When Ordinations at large did with other Corruptions creep into the Churches, a whole

whole *Synod* found it neceſſary not only to bear witneſs againſt that practice, but to declare ſuch Ordinations to be void and null, and the Ordainers liable to Cenſure. It is well obſerved by the Ingenuous Writer of the Hiſtory of the Council of *Trent* (i) that *in the Golden Times of Chriſtianity, no Perſons were Ordained but to a particular Miniſtry; but that this pious Inſtitution was ſoon Corrupted, Biſhops Ordaining men that had no Election by any Church.* This cauſed great Confuſion as the *Magdeburgenſian Hiſtorians* have noted. As a Remedy, the Council of *Calcedon* made a decree againſt all ſuch Ordinations. The Sixth *Canon* of that Synod declares, *That if any man ſhall be Ordained abſolutely,* that is to the Catholic without relation to a particular Church, *the Impoſition of Hands which he has received ſhall be null, and that he ſhall not Serve in the Church, to the diſhonour of them that have Ordained him.* This Decree was Confirmed by other *Synods* afterwards, ſo that it became a general Rule in the Church, that *no man ſhould be Ordained without a Title.* But the forementioned Hiſtorian (with many others) takes notice that this Rule was in proceſs of time perverted For whereas at firſt to have a *Title* was to have a *particular Church,* afterwards *to have a Title was to have Money.* The *Canons* of the Church of *England* will not permit any one to be *Ordained* without a *Title,* but they too much comply

with

(i) *Hiſt, Trid Conc L 6.*
p. 550.

with the *Papists* in allowing those to have *Titles* who have none such as the *Calcedonian* Council intended.

6. The impleaded *Ordinations* are contrary to the Judgment of our Eminent Divines, and to the practice of some of the best Reformed Churches. *Junius* (k) declares his Approbation of the mentioned *Canon* of the *Calcedon* Synod, 'And that since an Elder is not Ordained 'to the Ministry absolutely, but to the Mini-'ster of this or that Church in particular, it 'is fit that the Church should be concerned 'in the Ordination. And that in the Aposto-'lical Times in the Ordination of a Minister, 'there was first a *Cheirotonia* or Election by 'the People, and then a *Cheirothesia* or impo-'sition of hands ; That these two were al-'wayes joyned together as the Antecedent and 'Consequent. Mr: (l) *Cartwright* sayes that *after Election follows Ordination which is a So-lemn investing or putting a Minister into the Possession of that Office whereunto he was before Chosen.* To the like purpose does Dr *Whitaker* speak ; It is needless, and would be endless to heap up Testimonies concerning this, since it is a Common received opinion amongst our *Divines*, (we must always except *prelatical* ones) that *the Election of a Minister by the Church should precede his Ordination.* One of the Articles of the Ecclesiastical discipline of the French

(k) *Animadvers. in Bellarm. Contrum.* 5. *cap* 3. &c. 7.

(l) 2d *Reply p.* 272.

French Proteſtants, is, *Miniſters ſhall not be Ordained without Aſſigning them a particular Flock* So in the Kirk of *Scotland* one Article of their Polity is (m) *All Office bearers ſhould have their own particular Flocks, amongſt whom they Excerciſe their particular Charge*; as I find it Expreſſed by Mr *Calderwood.* That Learned (n) Author diſapproveth of the Impleaded Ordinations, becauſe they make a man to be a Miniſter only *Inpotentia,* but not *in actu.* Indeed Mr. *Rutherford* has ſuch ſtrange words as theſe, *It is preſuppoſed that A B is Ordained a Paſtor before the People can Elect him for their Paſtor.* Mr. *Hooker* replies to him that he finds *Bellarmine* ſpeaking juſt after that manner, which cauſed Dr. *Ames* to tell him, that he diſputed prepoſterouſly, and did ſet the Cart before the Horſe, when he placed Ordination before Election. But notwithſtanding Mr. *Rutherford* in that particular Notion deſerts the Common Proteſtant Doctrine, in another place he has theſe words, *A Paſtor is only the Paſtor of that Flock over which the Holy Ghoſt by the Churches Authority has ſet him as their Paſtor, yet ſo as when he Preacheth in another Congregation, he ceaſeth not to be a Paſtor, howbeit not the Paſtor of that Flock*; in ſaying which he yields the cauſe wholly as Mr. (o) Hooker

(m) *See the Hiſtory of the Church of Scotland.* p 105.

(n) *Altare damaſc.* p. 209.

(o) *Survey of Church Diſcipline* p. 2. p 61.

Hooker tells him. So then we are now agreed. I shall only add, that the *United Brethren* in *London* declare that Ordinarily, *None shall be Ordained to the work of the Ministry, but such as are called and chosen thereunto by a particular Church.* And that Learned Presbyterian Mr. *Gillespy* affirms, (†) That *Ordination ought to be given to him only who is Elected, and that because he is Elected.*

As for the other part of the Question, *Whether Ordination ought not to be performed in the presence of that Church where the Minister is to Serve?* The Answer is, That *Ordinarily* it ought to be The *Ordinations* which we read of in the Scripture were so. It a People who are remote from all Ministers fit to Ordain, desire one whom they have Elected to be Ordained for them in another Land, by a Solemn Separation of him to that Service of Christ, with Fasting and Prayer and Imposition of hands ; that's a rare case, and I know not why in such a case there may not be an Ordination though the Church is not (because they cannot be present. But if there are Elders in the place where the Minister is to dispense the Mysteries of the Gospel, for him to receive Ordination not in the presence of his Church, is irregular and contrary to Scripture Example. In the Primitive Times of Christianity, *Ordinations* were performed not only with the Consent, but *in the presence of*

the

(†) *Engl. pop. Cere. part.* 3. *chap.* 8.

the Church, yea, of the whole Church in which any *Pastor* was to *Preside*. *Cyprian* (*) affirms that no *Ordination* is rightly performed except the People to whom the Pastor is Ordained be present : He declares this to be according to the Doctrine and Practice of the Apostles. In the *third Century* it was thus practised both in the *Asian*, and in the *African* Churches. Thus was *Origen* (p) Ordained And another instead of *Narcissus* who was with-drawn from his Pastoral care of the Church in those days in *Jerusalem*.   The *Magdeburgesses* (q) in their *Ecclesiastical History* note that it any *Bishop* was to be Ordained they sent (not to Ministers in another Province a Thousand Miles distant but) to Neighbour Pastors for their Approbation, *Conveniebant fratres omnes* (say they) all the Brethren came together, and when the Election was over, they proceeded to an *Ordination* with the *Imposition of hands*, *Præsente universo populo*, in the presence of all the People Thus also it is amongst the Reformed Churches in *France*.   There was a Time when some young Scholars of the French Nation, having had their Education in the University of *Leyden* in *Holland* received Ordination from the hands of Dutch Divines, at which the *Presbyterians* in *France* were dissatisfyed : For which cause the *Synod* at *Gergeau*

(*) *L.* I. *Epist.* 4.
(p) *v Euseb. L* 6. c 8,.10.
(q) *Cent.* 3. *cap.* 6. *p. mihi.* 94, 102.

Gergean in the year 1601. made it one of their decrees, (*r*) *That Letters be written to the* Doctors *and Professors of Divinity, in the University* of Leyden, *intreating them not to Ordain the* French *Proposants Students in their University ; but when they have finished their Course of Theology, to send them into* France*, that here being called to the Ministry, they may receive imposition of hands in the face of our Churches.*

(r) *See Mr* Quicks *Synodicon.*

QUESTION XIV.

IS *the Practice of the Churches of* New-England *in granting Letters of Recommendation or Dismission from one Church to another according to Scripture and the Example of other Churches ?*

Answ It is so. See *Act.* 18 27. *Rom.* 16. 1, 2 That this was an usual Practice in the Churches in the Apostolical Times, is plain from 1 *Cor.* 16 3. *and* 3. 1. *Col.* 4. 10, 11. 3 *Joh.* 3. 8, 9, 10. This practice was continued in the Churches after the Apostolical Times. *Polycarp* in his Epistle to the Church at *Philippi* recommends *Crescens* with his Sister to their Communion, testifying that their Conversation had been blameless. The Greek Churches called such Letters as the Scriptures do *Systatick Epistles* or Letters of Recommen-

K   dation

dation. In the Latin Churches they were called *Literæ Communicatoriæ*. *Tertullian* call's them *Literas pacis*. That in the Primitive Times such Letters were in use may be seen in (s) *Baronius*. And that something of this nature was practised in the *Fourth Century* is manifest from a decree of the first Council in *Carthage* (t) That *no one shall Communicate in another Church without a Letter from the Bishop of his own Church*. *Nazianzene* in one of his *Orations* against *Julian* the Apostate speaks of these Letters And several Ancient *Synods* make mention both of *Literal Commendatitiæ*, and *Literæ dimissoriæ* And some of the Protestant Reformed Churches practice as the Churches of *New-England* do as to this matter. So in (u) *France*. And in *Holland* several of their *Synods* have Commended this practice of the Churches, that when persons remove from one Church to another in order to their partaking at the *Lords Table*, they should bring Letters Testimonial with them. Some of their greatest Divines have written in Defence of it. Dr. *Hornbeck* (w) Commends the Churches of *New-England* for this their Profession and practice. The famous *Gilbert Voetius* who has been esteemed the most Learned man in the World ; In Answer to
that

(s) *Tom.* 2. *Anno.* 142.
(t) *Magdeb. cent.* 4 c 9. *p.* 402.
(u) *v. La. Roque. p* ·145.
(w) *In Epist. ad Durcum. p.* 111.

that *Question, Whether in the Translation of Members from one Church to another, Letters Dimissory and Testimonial are not requisite?* Answers, (x) *Ita habet ordo Ecclesiasticus et laudabili more obtinet in Ecclesijs Belgicis.* Ecclesiastical order requires that it should be so. And this Laudable custom obtains in the *Dutch Churches.* He giveth diverse Reasons for it.

1. Such Letters will serve instead of a new Examination and Tryal which is necessary when persons are first Admitted into the Church.

2. Because otherwise Churches may be imprsed upon, so as to receive Members who are unfit, and it may be under offence in the Churches from whence they come.

3. To receive the Members of another Church without the Approbation of that Church to which they do belong, is the way to make difference in Churches, and to set them one against another. Thus that Learned man. Granting of *Letters Testimonial* was practised in the Churches in *Guernsey* when first Reformed : Their *Ecclesiastical Discipline* was the Composure of the famous *Thomas Cartwright* (as the Ministers in that *Island* assured me, when I had my Conversation amongst them many years since) Now one Article of their Discipline is, That *there shall not be received to the Lords Supper any one of other Parishes without Good Testimony from his Pastor, or of two of the Elders where there is no Minister.*

K 2   Al,

(x) *de pol. Eccles part. 1. c. 4. p. 67.*

Although it is true, that no Church ought to be made a Prison, It is nevertheless a Sin for any Church Member to leave that Church where the Providence of God has set him without just cause. It is a Violation of his Church Covenant. The removal of a Member from a Church does tend to the weakning of that Church If one may depart without just reason, why not another, and a third, and ten, twenty, and more, until the Church is in a manner dissolved. And therefore 'tis rational that if Members of Churches desire to remove their Relation to another Church, they should acquaint their own Church with their desires, and the reason thereof that so if they are justifiable, they may have a Loving *Dismission*, but if otherwise that they may be Convinced of their Error, and desist from their purpose. It is no sign of Wisdom for a man so to abound in his own sense, as not to ask the Advice of others (the Church especially to which he is related) in a matter of such moment *Prov*. 11. 14 & 12. 15. Letters of Dismission are requisite that so it may be known that his departure is not offensive. By the Letters in Controversy nothing else is intended, *but Letters Testimonial from some Church of Christ, or the Elders thereof, Concerning some of their Communion removing from them to another People, be it for lesser or longer Time.* The sorts of these Letters are diverse according to the Occasions of

of the person for whom they are written.
It is only for distinction sake that some are
called Letters of *Dismission*, others Letters of
Recommendation. For if we speak exactly, both
of them are Letters of *Recommendation*, containing some Testimonials for the party, and
both of them are Letters of *Dismission*, as signifying that he goeth with the consent of the
Church, whether it be with a purpose to return, or for continuance with those unto
whom he is going   In the *Heads of Agreement*
assented to by our Presbyterian and Congregational Brethren in *London*,   These are some,
*That a Visible professor joyned to a Particular
Church ought to continue steadfastly with the said
Church, and not forsake the Ministry and Ordinances there dispensed without an orderly seeking a
Recommendation to another Church*   Again they
say, *We ought not to Admit any one to be a
Member of our respective Congregations that has
joyned himself to another, without Endeavours of
Mutual Satisfaction of the Congregations concerned.*

QUESTION. XV.

IS not the asserting that a Pastor may Administer the Sacrament to another Church besides
his own Particular Flock, at the desire of that o-
ther Church, a declension from the First Principles of New-England, and of the Congregational
Way?

K 3   *Answ*

Answ. Not at all. For our *Platform of Church-Discipline* does not at all contradict it, but rather approve of it, *Chapt.* 15. S. 4. And some of the First Eminent Ministers in *New-England* have defended the lawfulness of such a practice. So Mr. *Norton* in his Answer to *Apollony*, Mr. *Shepard* of *Cambridge*, and Mr. *Allin* of *Dedham* in their Answer to Mr *Ball.* And my Father in a Letter of his to Mr. *Hooker*, bearing Date *Nov.* 6 1645. Giveth such Reasons for it as are not easie to be answered. Dr. *Goodwin* who was a Pillar amongst *Congregationals*, declares his Judgment fully in the Affirmative, and this not only in a Letter written not long before his Translation to Glory, of which I have elsewhere given an account, but in his Discourse of *Church Government*, in his fourth Volumn lately published, which was written long before that Letter, and wherein he shews that such an occasional Exercise of Ministerial Power in another Church at their Request will not Infer any such Jurisdiction as that which the *Presbyterian Brethren* plead for. We shall for the satisfaction of those that have not that Book of the *Doctors*, cause his words to be Transcribed. He thus speaks, (*y*) It is one thing that there may Occasionally be an Exercising of an Elders Power in another Congregation, 'and it is another thing that it 'should be assumed and challenged, which is 'the thing that remains further to be proved

6 b.

(*y*) B. 5. Ch. 10 p. 232.

'by the Presbyterial Divines. As it is one
'thing for a Child under Age, tho' he should
'not Govern himself, to have Liberty to chuse
'a Guardian for the Time, but it is another
'thing that a Company of men should af-
'sume to be his Guardians for ever. It will
'be one thing for a Corporation to send to a-
'nother Corporation for their Recorder, a
'man skilful in the Law, to perform the Of-
'fice of a Recorder with a Jury at their Seffi-
'on, they now wanting one, or there falling
'out a Case of difficulty, wherein their own
'does need Affiftance ; but it will be another
'thing for the Recorders of several Corporati-
'ons in a County to go and challenge by ver-
'tue of Affociation, and the Common Law of
'Communion in the Kingdom, a conftant
'power of Jurifdiction to be Exercifed over
'them.

    'And in this cafe the Communion of
'Churches in refpect of Members *Qua* Mem-
'bers, and of Elders, *Qua* Elders anfwer one
'another, according to our principles. For as
'the Members of another Church, if they
'come to a Particular Church, and are recei-
'ved by their Confent by them, and fo for that
'Time become as one body with them, by
'vertue whereof they receive the Sacrament a-
'mongft them, as being for this act incorpora-
'ted and as one bread with them occafion-
'ally, in this do not receive meerly and fimply
'as Members of another Church, diftinctly &c.
'a part confidered, altho' by vertue of their be-
'ing Members of another Church, but they are

'thereby for that Time occafionally received
'into that Church *ad tantum* fo far as to En-
'joy fuch and fuch a priviledge, fo as the Sa-
'crament in this, is not faid to be given to the
'Members of two Churches apart confidered,
'but to one Church as thus making one, tho'
'upon a diff'ring refpect ; and fo it is alfo
'in their receiving Elders (if we may
'make that fuppofition) to perform Acts
'of Elderfhip occafionally, they do it not in
'this fingle and apart Confideration that
'they are fimply Elders of other Churches,
'as if confidered only as fuch they may
'make a Confiftory met out of this Church
'to be over this Church, and fo Excom-
'municate, but they come to and are pre-
'fent in and with that Church being called
'by them, and received as Elders for that
'Act, and for that Time as one with them,
'fo as the Acts which they do perform are
'Acts of that Church, or of Elders in that
'Church, and are not to be confidered as
'Acts of other Elders that have no power
'over that Church. Thus far Dr. *Goodwin*.
And that this accords with the Judgment of
Congregational Divines, and was alfo practifed
in the next Ages to the Apoftles, when *Poly-*
carp Paftor of the Church in *Smyrna* adminif-
ftred the Sacrament to the then Church of
Saints in *Rome*, I have more fully declared in
an Anfwer to this *Queftion*, which was printed in the Year, 1693. And thus it was practifed in the Churches of *New-England* in their
b. gin

beginning Times! For when Mr. *Wilson*, Paſtor of the only Church then in *Boston*, was abſent from his Flock in a Voyage for *England*, Mr *Phillips*, Paſtor of the Church in *Watertown*, adminiſtred the Lords Supper to the Church in *Boſton*. This was above threeſcore years ſince. And thus did Mr. *Eliot*, (a zealous man for the Order of the Goſpel, practiſed in the *Platform* of Diſcipline). practice forty years ago in the *Indian Churches*.

QUESTION. XVI.

IS it a Duty for *Chriſtians in their* Prayers to make uſe of the words of that which is Commonly called the Lords Prayer?

Anſw. It cannot be proved that this is a duty. The *Queſtion* is not whether it is *Lawful* to make uſe of thoſe words in Prayer. No man can rationally doubt, but that the words in that as well as the words of other Prayers in the Scripture may be made uſe of in our Addreſſes to Heaven. The Rigid *Separatiſts* will not deny this. Mr. *Aynſworth* ſayes, (a) *We hold it Good and Holy to uſe aright any of the Lords Prayers, or any words of Scripture, or thoſe or any of thoſe Petitions taught us in* Matth. 6. *or* Luk. 11. *in the words of either*

(a) *v* Mr. *Pagets Arrow againſt Separation.* p. 4, 63.

ither *Evangelist, or other words as the Spirit of God which helps us to Pray, leadeth us to any of them* Likewise Mr. *Robinson* (b) who was a *Rigid Separatist* until Dr. *Ames* convinced him of his Error therein, He sayes, *We hold it Lawful to use those very words in our Prayers, all, or any part of them, if we be thereunto Guided by the Holy Spirit in whom we must always Pray, and by whose help we must make our Requests unto God.* Doubtless then Congregational men will concede as much as this cometh to. Mr. *Jeremiah Burroughs* (a famous Divine of the Congregational Perswasion) once when he Preached his *Expository Lectures* was prevented from coming to the Assembly exactly at the Hour appointed, If he should at that time have inlarged in Prayer as he usually did, the Auditors would have been detained longer then they expected. Nor was he willing to begin his Exposition without any Prayer at all, he therefore began it with only Praying in the words of *the Lords Prayer.* This report I believe ; for my most Dear and Honoured Friend Dr. *William Bates,* late Pastor of a Church in *Hackney* near *London* (whom for Honours sake I mention) assured me that he was then present and an *Ear Witness* of what I have now related But the Question is, Whether this is *necessary:* Not whether a Minister *may* without Sin make use of the words of the

Lords

(b) In his Answer to Mr. Bernard
p. 469.

Lords Prayer, but whether he *Ought* to do it, and Confequently fhall be guilty of *Sin* if he does it *not*. The *Question* being fo ftated we defend the *Negative*. Let it be confidered.

1. That our Saviours words are, *After this manner pray ye*. Mat. 6. 9. Wnence *Auftin* (c) concludes that Chrift taught his Difciples not what *words* they fhould ufe in Prayer, but what *things* they fhould pray for. To the fame purpofe does *Beda* fpeak. And this alfo is the fenfe of *Ca'vin, Mufculus, Pifcator, Bertram*, and of *Grotius* himfelf, that our Saviour did not intend that *His Difciples were bound to re-cite thofe words in Prayer, nor would He tye them to the ufe of Syllables*. Nor indeed is it proba-ble that our Lord in the midft of his Sermon would prefcribe a Form of Words to His Difciples. Whence Mr. *Jofeph Mede* (a great Conformift) concludes, (d) That *when thofe words were firft uttered, the Difciples underftood not that their Mafter intended it for a Form of Prayer, but for a Pattern or Example only*. He that prays for any thing not contained in that *Platform* of Prayer, does not pray *after that manner*, but he that does with Faith pray for the things comprehended therein, although he fhould not ufe one Expreffion in it, but other words importing that fenfe, does truly *Pray after that manner*. It is P eaded that in *Luke* the words are *When you pray, fay* ; but that may well be interpreted not as intending fay

thefe

(c) *Lib. de Magiftro. cap.* 1.
(d) *See his Works. Fol.* 2.

these words, but *these things* in your prayers : So does *Grotius* give the sence of them. When *Moses* was charged, *Thou shalt say* unto *Pharaoh,* &c. *Exod* 4. 22. He did not think that he was obliged to say those *very words,* only to Express that *thing:* Nor did he in delivering his Message tye himself to those words and syllables. The like may be here affirmed. Moreover, most of those that do *Say the Lords Prayer,* do not say as 'tis in *Luke*

2 The two Evangelists in their Reciting that Prayer have not the same words. Whence we conclude that it was given only as a *Platform* or *Directory* for Prayer, and not as a *Form* which we may not vary from. In *Luke* there is no *Amen* concluding the Prayer nor any *Doxology,* besides the words both in the fourth and in the fifth Petition are not just the same words with those in *Matthew.* Now if the meaning of *Pray after this manner,* and of *when you pray, say,* is, that we are in duty bound to use those words and syllables as a Form, whose Form must we follow ? whether that of *Matthew,* which is part of Christ's Sermon on the Mount ? or that in *Luke* which was taught the Disciples in another place, and on another occasion, near upon a year and half after the Former ? Dr. *Lightfoot* (*d*) tells us that the Jews concluded their Prayers in Synagogues, and private Houses with saying *Amen;* but that they never said *Amen* in the Temple, but instead thereof, they concluded

with

(*d*) *in vol. 2. fol.* 1138.

with saying thele Words, *Bleſſed be Name of the Glory of his Kingdom forever and ever.* I remember a Jewiſh *Rabbi* ſays that thoſe words were the uſual Prayer of their Father *Jacob*, but the *Doctor* thinks that the *Doxology* is omitted in *Luke*, and added in *Matthew*, to inſtruct us that we ſhould uſe this Form, both in Publick and in Private. Yet this Anſwers not the Queſtion, which of theſe Forms is to be uſed; which of them in Publick, and which in Private? If we muſt keep exactly to the *Jewiſh* mode of worſhip, the Form in *Matthew* muſt not be uſed in the *Cathedral* which anſwers to the Temple, becauſe it concludes with *Amen.* Nor muſt the Form in *Luke*, becauſe it wants the *Doxology*, which is peculiar to the Temple. The Goſpel does not require nor approve of *Indaizing* in Chriſtians.

3 That Common Argument, however ſlighted by Mr. *Paget* (e) which mary have produced to prove that the Formal uſage of the Lords Prayer, is not Commanded, deſerves further Conſideration, *viz* becauſe *then it would be unlawful to vary at all from thoſe words as a Syllables.* When it is ſaid, *Pray thus,* and *when you Pray, ſay,* thoſe words of our Saviour are not a *Permiſſion,* but an abſolute *Commandment. When you Pray,* that is, *Whenever you pray.* As, *when you give Alms,* is as much as to ſay, *when ever you give Alms.* Thus *when ſoever a Chriſtian prayes,* he muſt pray after that manner which Chriſt in his Sermon

L

an

on the Mount prescribed.   If therefore the meaning of *Pray thus*, is, use these very words, it would not be Lawful at any time to vary from them.   Which no man will be so unreasonable as to affirm.   It would be less proper for a Christian in his Closet to speak in the plural number.   Indeed the Superstitious Jews made a *Canon* that their *Compendious Prayer*, which they call *Majan q. d* 'a *Fountain Prayer* and require their Disciples to say it Eighteen times every day, shall be Expressed in the plural number, though he that sayes it has no man with him, and they make him Guilty of &c. that shall Pray that Prayer in the singular number though in his Closet, because he must never look on himself as Separated from the Synagogue.   But does any man believe, that if a Christian shall say, give *me* my daily bread, forgive *my* debts, lead not *me* into Temptation, deliver *me* from evil, that he offends by not speaking plurally in the very Syllables of the Lords Prayer ?   It would be so, if the design of the precept were to tye us up to Words and Syllables.

.4. There are few of those who use the *Lords Prayer*, that keep to the words either of *Matthew* or of *Luke* in their saying of it.   For in the *Fifth Petition* they vary therefrom The words in *Matthew* are, *Forgive us our debts as we forgive our debtors*, Math. 6. 12 The words in *Luke* are, *Forgive us our Sins For we also forgive every one that is indebted to us*, Luk. 11. 4. When as they that say th

he Lords Prayer use the words which are in
the *Liturgy,* viz *Forgive us our Trespasses as we
forgive them that trespass against us.* It will be
said, that is the same *thing* though not the same
words with the other. But this is to give up
the cause, since our Question is not concerning
things but *words.* Moreover, by this small
alteration of the words a Great Truth, viz.
That our Sins are our Debts, is lost. *Cyprian*
is justly blamed for making a little change in
the *Sixth Petition,* for he expresseth it, *Ne pa-
tiaris nos induci &c. Suffer us not to be led
into Temptation,* whereby a great and myste-
rious Truth respecting the Activity of Providence in Leading men into Temptation is
obscured. They that pretend they are bound
in Conscience to use the *Lords Prayer* as a
Form, and so to keep exactly to the words
therein contained, are not able to Extricate
themselves from this Argument against
them. Nor can I give any reason why they
express the *Fifth Petition* as they commonly
do, excepting this, that they have taken their
use of the Lords Prayer, not out of the *Bible*
but out of the *Common Prayer Book.*

5. It cannot be proved that either Christ or
his Apostles did use this Prayer as a Form.
A most Heavenly Prayer made by our Saviour, is recited in the 17*th* of *John,* but He did
not conclude with the words of this prayer:
We find in *Acts* 1. 24. And in *Act,* 4. 24.
That the Apostles prayed in Church-Meetings,
but not that they did either begin or conclude

with

with the recitation of the Lords Prayer. *Durandus* (f) boldly affirms, That the Apostles Consecrated the *Eucharist*, by repeating the words of Institution, & super-adding the Lords Prayer. And that *Peter* did at first so Celebrate that Ordinance in the Oriental Parts where he Resided for the space of four years. I doubt not but that this is as true, as what he further says, that afterwards that Apostle caused *three Prayers more to be added to the Mass* There is no more proof that the Apostles any of them used to say the Lords Prayer, then there is that the *Liturgy* fathered on *James* was written by him; the vanity whereof has been sufficiently discovered by our Protestant Divines. That Incomparable Divine and *Casuist*, Dr. *Ames*, (†) judgeth that we may conclude that the Lords Prayer was not given as a Form, but as a Platform, *because the Scripture says nothing of the Apostles so using it.* Neither do the Apostles or Evangelists in any of their Writings Exhort Christians unto the formal usage of that Holy Directory for prayer. Nor do we read any thing of that matter in the next Age after the Apostles. *Eusebius* (g) has recorded an Excellent Prayer made by *Polycarp* when he Suffered *Martyrdom*; but although he prayed after that manner which the Lords Prayer requires, there is not one sentence of that prayer in his. *Justin Martyr* gives an account of what was

(f) *Rationale Divin.* Li. 4 c. 1, & cap 47.
(†) *Cas. Consc* L. 4. c. 17.
(g) L. 4 c. 15.

was practised in the Assemblies of Christians in those days, *viz.* of their Reading the Scriptures, Preaching thereon, Prayers, Administration of Baptism and the Lords Supper, but has not the least hint of their using to repeat the Lords Prayer, which had it then been Customary, no doubt he would have mentioned it as he does some other things which were deviations from the Apostolical practice, particularly that of sending the *Eucharist* to such as were absent. It is true, that in the *third Century*, the Lords prayer was used in some of the Assemblies of Christians, yet not in all of them, only when the *Communicants* were by themselves alone : They never repeated that prayer if any that were only *Catechumens* hapned to be present. Nor might (*h*) such use it until they were baptized. They supposed it unlawful for Unregenerates to call God their Father. The Writings of *Austin* (*i*) and *Chrysostom* and others of the Ancients have made this indisputable. There is an expression in *Tertullian* (*k*) from whence some have gathered, that in those days Christians did not *Conclude* but *Begin* their prayers with *the Lords Prayer.* Nevertheless, they did not think it necessary. It

L 3   is

(*h*) *Hanc orationem baptizati orant*
         August *Epist.* 54.
(*i*) *In Matth Homil* 18. *and*
         2 *Cor. Homil.* 2.
(*k*) *Præmissa Legitima oratione.*
   Tertull. de orat. p. 659.

is evident that *Origen* did sometimes use this prayer; but without an opinion of its being necessary. For when he writes concerning a method of prayer, he adviseth to begin and end with *Doxologies*: but he does not advise to begin or to end with the Lords prayer. *Clemens Alexandrinus* concludes his last Book of *Pedagogy* with prayer, yet not with the *Lords Prayer*. This enervates what Mr. Richard Ward and other object, *viz.* That if the Lords prayer, was given only to be a rule, and not enjoyned as a form, then Christians for 1500 years together did not understand the true meaning of *Mat.* 6 9. But suppose that an hundred years after the Apostles were all dead, *this Formality* had been generally practised, we could not from thence infer, that it was so in their dayes. For *Innovations* and *Declensions* from the *Primitive Purity* were soon brought in unawares amongst the Churches. In *Tertullians* Time, they *Prayed towards the East.* *Origen* also adviseth it; but the Apostles never gave that Advice In those dayes they used *Exorcisms, signing with the Cross* and *Chrism* in Baptism. All which thing were Corruptions in Religion, and are now rejected by most of the Reformed Churches In those Times also, they put especial respect upon *Wednesdays* and *Fridays,* which in *Tertullian* are called *Stationum dies.* Because Christ was Sold on a *Wednesday,* and Crucified on a *Friday* they would have more devotion on those then on other dayes in the week. These were

Ecc

Early Superstitions. And although we read nothing of their keeping the Feast of *Chrift's Nativity* for more than an hundred years after this; nevertheleſs, *Whitſunday* and *Pentecoſt* was obſerved in Commemoration of the deſcent of the Holy Ghoſt on the Apoſtles. Alſo *Lent* and *Eaſter* were accounted Sacred Times. The obſervation of *Eaſter* was as ancient as *Polycarp*, who was the Diſciple of the Apoſtle *John.* Preſently after *Polycarp*, Chriſtians uſed every year to obſerve a day in Commemoration of the *Death Dayes* which they called *the Birth Dayes* of their Martyrs. I have mentioned theſe particulars to ſhew that the Argument from the *practice* of Churches after the Apoſtles Dayes, is not concluſive except it can be proved that the *Scripture* does warrant ſuch a practice, and then it is *ex abundanti*, recommended to us, 1 *Cor.* 11. 16.

6. Other Arguments beſides that of *Ancient Cuſtom* which are commonly alledged for uſeing *the Lords Prayer* as a *Form*, do not carry Conviction with them. It is pleaded, that our Prayers are Imperfect, when as this Form contains in it all that we are to pray for, therefore to make up *the Defects* of our Prayers, we muſt ſubjoyn this. To which has been replyed, that the *Decalogue* does contain in it, all the Duties which God requires of men, *Matth* 22. 40. But it does not therefore follow that Miniſters ſhould conclud their Imperfect Sermons with a *Recitation* of the *Ten Commandments.* No more are they bound to

to a *Repetition* of *the Lords Prayer*, at the
Conclution of their own imperfect ones.
Moreover, we may not think that *Words and
Syllables* will make amends for the *Defect* of
our Prayers; for that is (as shall be further
said) to give to them what is proper to the
Merit and *Intercession* of the Lord Jesus Christ.
It is also pretended that every *Rabbi* or *Master*
amongst the Jews delivered a *Form of Prayer*,
to his Disciples. That *John Baptist* did so:
And that in *Conformity* hereunto, the Disciples
Petitioned Christ to give them a *Form*, which
he granted their desires in : And that he took
every Sentence of this which we call the *Lords
Prayer* out of the Jews Common *Prayer-Book*
at that time used amongst them, and willed his
Disciples to *use it as a Form*. Thus do some
say. And all this is sooner said than proved.
Some have told us of things in the *Jewish
Rituals* which others could never find there.
Baronius, Casauben and many besides, say, that
it was usual amongst the Jews to wash their
feet before they sat down to eat the Passover,
and that therefore what is recorded, *Joh. 13. 5.*
was nothing but a Jewish custom used at the
Passover Yet *Buxtorf* (who was as much
conversant in the Writings of the Jews as any
man in the world) says, that *if a man reads
over all their Ritual Books, and the whole Talmud
besides, he will not find any such thing therein.*
Other particulars relating to the Administration
of the *Lords Supper*, are by *Genebrard, Scaliger*,
(with many more) pretended to be in imita-
tion

tion of what is in the *Jewish Rituals*, whom the Learned Reader may see refuted by *Buxtorf* in his Differtation *de Cœna Dominica*. The like to this may be affirmed with refpect to the Subject before us. But fuppofing (which yet remains to be demonftrated) the Difciples were to ufe this prayer as a Form whilft they continued under the *Jewish Pedagogy*, it cannot from thence be concluded that Believers under the *New-Teftament* are bound fo to ufe it. There are fome Lerrned men that do allow the Lords Prayer to have been a *prefcribed Form*, that do not think it to be defigned for the perpetual ufe of the Church as fuch, but only for a *Temporary Form*. And that after our Lords Refurrection and Afcenfion, they fhould no longer ufe it as a Form, becaufe therein is no expref's mention of the name of Chrift, nor asking Bleffings for his fake, nor afcribing praifes to God through him, which after his accomplifhing the work of Redemption, ought to be. Thus do they interpret that Scripture, *Joh.* 16 24. However it does not follow that it a *Form* were *proper* and needful for the *Jews*, that fuch things are neceffary for *Chriftians* in the dayes of the Gofpel, wherein there is a more plentiful effufion of the fpirit of prayer. *Zech.* 12. 10 *We fay not that all Forms are un'awful.* No doubt but that a man who has not the gift of prayer, had better make ufe of a *Form* of his own compofing or taken out of fome good Book, (but I would not advife to take one out of the *Mafs-Book*) to worfhip God

God with, in his Family, then not to have any Religious Worship at all therein. But if that man shall afterwards be blessed with a *Gift of Prayer*, for him to tye himself to a Form is (as useth to be said) like as if one that has used Crutches whilst he was weak, should continue to use them after he has gained strength. What *Liturgies* the *Jews* had whilest they were yet the Church of God, we know not. Nor is there any great Credit to be given to what their *Rabbins* who are made up *of Fables*, shall think meet to tell us. Some of themselves confess that Forms of Prayer were not always used by their Fathers. *Saubertus* in his late Learned *Academical Disquisitions*, Cites a passage of *R. Bechai*, (m) who sayeth, *That from the time of Moses until the Great Sanedrim, there was no ordinary Form of Prayer amongst the Israelites, but every man made a prayer for himself, according to what knowledge and gift of utterance he was endued with.* If the Jews had Prayer Books of *Humane Composure* in our Saviours Time, (as our *Liturgical* men are perswaded) it is too much boldness to Conjecture that the Lord borrowed the Petitions in the *Lords prayer* from them. What though *Grotius*, (*) and others find Expressions like those, in Jews Prayer Books ? It does not necessarily follow that they were taken from thence. Dr. *Lightfoot*

(m) *V. Saubert Palæstra p.* 123.
(*) *v.* Dr. Taylors *ductor dubit.*
Lib. 2. *c.* 3. *R* 15.

foot (n) chargeth the Jews with *Filching* out of the Gospel, particularly that they have Stolen those words, *Thy Kingdom come,* and those, *Lead us not into Temptation,* and inserted them into their *Liturgies.* This seems more probable, then that the Lord should take his Prayer out of their Service Books. It was counted Blasphemy in *Celsus,* when he affirmed that Christ borrowed many of his Divine Notions out of *Plato* Mr. *Boyse* mentions an horrid Assertion of Dr. *Combers* in his pretended Answer to Mr. *Clarksons* unanswerable discourse of *Liturgies,* viz. *That our Saviour was so afraid of Innovation as to take every Sentence of the Lords prayer out of the Jewish Forms then in use.* In that degenerate Age was he afraid to teach any thing that would seem *New* to them! How then did some who heard him Preach, say, *What new Doctrine is this?* Mar. 1. 27. Was the Lord who did so often reprove them for their Formality in Worship, *Afraid* of *Innovation* if they should change their *Vain Conversation received by Tradition from their Fathers?* Was that admirable *Directory* for prayer which none but he who is the *Wisdom of God* could be the Author of, all borrowed out of Jewish *Common Prayer-Books,* devised by no man knows who? *Credat Judæus Apella.*

7. That many have *Superstitiously* abused this blessed portion of Scripture, cannot be denied. They have set up the *Lords Prayer* in

the

(n) *Joh.* 1. *p.* 1003.

the room of *Christ* himself, imagining that God will accept of their other Petitions for the sake of their repeating this *Form*, as if that would *Sanctifie* and make amends for the *defects* in their prayers, which to do belongs to the *Mediator*, nor can any thing else do it. The Judicious *Alting* (o) giveth this caution, *That in using the Lords Prayer men should be careful of Superstition in thinking that there is a Latent Efficacy in Words and Syllables.* Papists will say their *Pater Noster* more often in an hour, then the Jews do their *Majan* prayer in a day, superstitiously dreaming that the pronouncing of those Letters and Syllables will save them. One of the most moderate (†) and ingenuous of their Writers speaks thus, *Both rising & going to bed, sitting down and rising from board, and going about any particular action or business; I would have all good Christians to say the* Pater. Noster. *It is (sayes he) the only Prayer that I use at every place, at all times, and upon every accident; and instead of changing, I use often Repetition of it.* Thus speaks a Roman Catholick. Nor are all who call themselves *Protestants*, altogether free from *Superstition* in this matter. Many of them are (as Mr. *Fenner* speaks) in their saying the Lords Prayer, Guilty of *Syllabical Idolatry.* There are some make a *Charm* of those Letters and Syllables. What is it better when persons are Judged to be either innocent or guilty of the Crime of *Witchcraft*

(o) *Theol. problem p.* 740.
(†) Montaigne *Essayes. Ch.* 56. *p.* 172.

craft according as they have power to say or not to say the *Lords Prayer* ? Whether it was Inftituted to be a *Form* or no, I am fure it was never Inftituted to Try who are *Witches* : Nor can the Inability of fome Perfons to pronounce thofe Words and Syllables, who can pronounce any other, proceed from natural caufes, but from the operation of *Dæmons.* Nor is there certainty in the Experiment. *Glanvil* (as I remember) confeffeth that this kind of *Ordeal* is fallible. I fhall take notice of but one Allegation more : It is pretended that our Saviour has *Obliged us to a Form of Words* in the Adminiftration of *Baptifm,* and of *the Lords Supper:* And then why not as well to a Form of words in Prayer ? If it were as is objected, there is no confequence in the Argument : It does not at all follow that if there are fome Forms of Divine Inftitution, that then the Lords Prayer was given as a Form Moreover, although it is Lawful and Commendable in Miniftring Baptifm to keep to the words of Inftitution in *Matth.* 28 19. Yet neither is this Commanded, but an Agreement in fence is fufficient. For it is evident that the Apoftles did not alwayes keep to that *Form. Act* 2. 38 & 4. 16. & 10 48 & 19.5. This is fo manifeft, as that *Aquinas* confeff.th it, only he fuppofeth that the Apoftles had by Revelation a particular difpenfation for their not keeping to the prefcibed Form Dr. *Lightfoot* fayes, that when the Apoftles Bap ifed Jews, it was *in the Name of Jefus,* becaufe the great Controverfy amongft

M   them

them was, *Whether Jesus of Nazareth was the true Messiah*; but that when they Baptised the Gentiles where that Controversy had no footing, they Baptised *into the Name of the Father, Son and Holy Spirit.* The Greek & the Latin Church did not keep exactly to the same Form of words in their Miniftring that Holy Ordinance. In the Greek Church fometimes they faid, *I Baptise,* fometimes, *Be thou Baptised* but their ufual Form was, *This Servant of Chrift is Baptised:* Yea they intermixed fome words of their Belief with the words of Inftitution in their Adminiftring Baptifm. Thus *Juftin Martyr* declares, that *Wafhing with Water is performed in the Name of the Father of all things, and our Lord God, and of our Saviour Jefus Chrift, and of the Holy Spirit.* Again, he fayes, *in the Name of Chrift who was Crucified under Pontius Pilate.* Amongft the Latins they did not keep to the Words and Syllables of the Inftitution. For *Cyprian* fayes, *In nomine,* in the Name, but *Tertullian, In nomen,* INTO the Name, (which is moft agreeable to the Original.) And in another place he does not mention *Name* in the Form ufed in Baptifm, but fayes, *Into the Father, Son and Holy Spirit.* This variation as to words as long as the fence and defign was the fame, they thought was no variation from the Precept. Of this Judgment are *Cartwright, Martinius,* and *Voetius* amongft our Modern Writers. The like is to be affirmed with refpect to the *Lords Supper.* Notwithftanding the words of *Inftitution* are recited by
three

three of the *Evangelists*, and by *Paul* to the *Corinthians*, nevertheless they all as to some words differ, but agree in the Substance of what is by each of them related, which shews that we are not in the Administration of the Holy Supper, limitted to the use of *alwayes the same Words & syllables*. It is clear and manifest from *Austin*, and others of the Ancients that there was in those dayes a great variety used in the *Consecration* of the Elements. Now if the using the very words of Institution in Ministring the Sacraments is not Commanded, much less are we Commanded to use the words Expressed in *our Lords Director, for Prayer*. We conclude then that since the use of those words *as a Form* is only a thing *Indifferent*, and not necessary, or a Commanded duty ; when the case is so circumstanced that it cannot be done without *Offence*, it is rather a duty and will be most pleasing to Christ not to use it as a Form. It is a sound Principle which some of the *School men* have maintained. *Etiam Spiritualia non necessaria sunt fugienda, si exijs Scandalum oritur. Hos.* 2. 16. *I Cor.* 10. 32

I shall only add, that *Biddle* (the notorious *Socinian*) having asserted, that our Saviour Prescribed the Lords Prayer to be used as a Form by his Disciples, Dr. *Owen* proposeth several *Queries* for him or any on his behalf to Answer ; and amongst others these, *Whether the asserting this Form of Words to be used, has not confirmed many in their Atheistical Blaspheming the Holy Spirit of God, and His Grace in*

the

the Prayers of His People ? And whether the Repetition of these words after men have been long Praying for the things contained in them, as the manner of some is ; be not so Remote from any Pretence or Colour of warrant in the Scriptures, as that it is in plain termes Ridiculous Thus Dr. Owen in his Answer to *Biddle.* p. 669.

QUESTION XVII.

MAY *the Churches under the Presbyterian and Congregational Discipline maintain Communion with one another, notwithstanding their differing Sentiments as to Church Government ?*

Answ. They may and ought to do so. In the Apostolical Churches there were as great and greater differences in Judgment then are those between the Brethren of these two Perswasions ; who nevertheless did maintain a Christian Communion with each other, as it was their Duty to do. *Rom.* 14. 1, 2. *Phil.* 3. 15, 16. They have been *Confessors,* and Fellow-Sufferers for bearing witness to the same Cause of Truth, which should Endear them to each other. In matters of Faith they all agree. Yea, and in the *Substantials of Church Order* They all say, that there ought to be nothing in the Worship of God, besides what Himself has appointed. No Officers in the Church, nor Sacraments, nor Censure sures but what are the Institutions of Christ. A moderate Presbyterian, and a solid Congregational man agree in so many things, and differ in so few and small things, that it would be a shame for them to divide and break Communion about them. A man that giveth himself to Reading and Searching after Truth, may in a few years time, see cause to differ from himself as much as a *Presbyterian* and *Congregational man* differ from one another. The *Provincial Assembly* of *London* in their Treatise of the Divine *Right of the Gospel Ministry.* Part 1. p.191. Speak respectfully of the *New England Platform of Church Discipline,* although they concur not therewith in some particulars, they say concerning the Ministers of *New England,* that they *agree with them wholly in the same Confession of Faith, and in many things of the greatest concernment in the matter of Church Discipline. And that those things wherein we differ, are not of such consequence as to make a Schism between us.* They further add, that *they can truly say as their Brethren in* New-England *do in the Preface to the Platform,* (which Preface was written by Mr. *Cotton,* and approved of by other Elders) that *it is far from us so to attest the Discipline of Christ as to detest the Disciples of Christ.* Dr *Arrowsmith* sometimes *Regius Professor* of Divinity in the University of *Cambridge,* notwithstanding his being a Presbyterian, calls the Ministers in *New-England, Fratres nostros jure nobis dilectissimi;* Our Brethren deservedly most dear unto us. *V. Tactica sacra. p.* 115. The Godly

M 3   Learned

Learned Mr. *Rutherford* has declared, that if the *Congregationals* would all come up to what Mr. *Cotton* asserts in his Book of the *Keyes of the Kingdom*, he would meet them half way. Mr. *Baxter*, not long before he went to his *Everlasting Rest*, said to me, If all *Independents* were like *New-England Independents*, we should soon be one. Our Congregational Brethren in *England* who met at the *Savoy*, Anno 1658. Have this for the last Article of their Discipline, *Churches gathered and walking according to the mind of Christ, judging other Churches (though less pure) to be true Churches, may receive to occasional Communion with them, such Members of those Churches as are credibly testified to be Godly, and to live without offence.* The practice of the Churches in *New-England* ha's been according to this profession. For we have received to our Communion those that have come to us with Testimonials from Presbyterian Ministers in *England*, and divers that have come to us from *Scotland* Yea, and some *French Refugees* of whose sincere Piety we have had Testimonials And (which is more) several worthy Ministers known to be of the Presbyterian Judgment who came to us from *England*, particularly Mr. *Morton* and Mr. *Baily*, were received among us with the greatest respects that the Elders and Churches in *New-England* could manifest towards them. And whereas they did scruple a Re-ordination by Imposition of hands (which is usual in these Churches) that was not urged upon them, but they were established in the

Churches who Elected them with fasting and prayer, without any laying on of hands. Mr. *cotton* not long before his departure to a better World, drew up some *proposals* for the *Acccommodation and Union* of these two Reforming Perswasions, in which his Spirit was very much ingaged. My most dear Brother *Samuel Mather* (who was well known to the Churches in *New England* above forty years ago, and after that in *England* and in *Ireland,* where he ended his days) not long before he finished his Course, wrote a small Book which beareth the Title of *Irenicum,* or an *Essay for Union ;* wherein he shows how inconsiderable the Differences are between those of the *Presbyterian and Congregational Judgment,* and that they may without any selling of Truth to purchase peace, mutually own and give the Right Hand of Fellowship to each other, as true Churches and Ministers of Jesus Christ, that they should lay aside all their Animosities, and remember that Golden Rule, Rom. 14. 3. *Let not him that Eateth, despise him that Eateth not, and let not him that Eateth not, judge him which Eateth, for God has received him.* So let not him who depends on the way of Classical Subordination, despise him that dependeth not, and let not him that dependeth not, judge him that dependeth, for the Lord has received them both.

Amongst those who go under the name of *Congregational,* there is a variety of apprehension in some *Disciplinary Controversies.* Some of them have thought that no Children should
be

Be admitted to Baptism whose Parents are not admitted to the Lords Table. This was the opinion of our Learned Mr. *Chauncey*, who was many years Præsident of the Colledge, and of Mr. *Davenport*, and some few others of the first Ministers in these Churches. But Mr. *Cotton*, my Father *Mather*, Mr. *Norton*, Mr. *Rogers*, Mr. *Mitchel*, and the generality of our *New-England* Divines were for a greater Latitude as to the subject of Baptism. Some esteem none to be Members of the *Visible Church*, excepting those that belong to *Particular Churches*: So Mr. *Hooker*, Mr. *Stone*, and most of our Ministers. But in this the generality of *Congregationa's* in *England* vary from them. They suppose that *all the men in the world, who deserve the name of Christians,* or that make a profession of the true Religion, and do not destroy that profession by any Error in Judgment, or Scandal in Conversation, are the *Catholick Visible Church*, of which number there are many who are not in full Communion with any particular *Instituted Church*. Some limit Baptism to Membership in a particular Church. So has it been with us in *New-England* for the most part. But other *Congregationals* differ from us in this point. Dr. *Goodwin* has strenuously asserted, that a *Particular Church* is the Subject of that Ordinance of the *Lords Supper*, but not of *Baptism*. And of this Judgment were Dr. *Owen*, and Mr. *Greenhil*, as both of them did many years since in Letters I received from them, signifie to me; & Dr *Owen* in divers of his printed Books, declares
that

he was so perswaded   So that they who go under the name of *Congregational* must withdraw
Communion from one another as well as from
Presbyterians, if differing sentiments about *Disciplinary Questions,* be a sufficient ground for dis-
union and separation.   Dr. *Ames* was *Congregational,* highly approving of the Churches in
New-England; and purposing to have ended his
dayes amongst them.   On his Death-bed (as
one that was then with him has publickly testified) he declared that if there were any Churches, in the World whom God would own, they
were such as those in *New-England.*   And altho'
Gangræna says, that then it was a mercy that
Learned *Ames* lived no longer, better men than
he will not say so.   Dr. *Twiss* was Presbyterian,
nevertheless, there was an Endearedness between
Ames and him.   Mr. *Marshal* and Mr. *Strong*
Loved as Brethren notwithstanding the former
was Presbyterian, and the Latter Congregational. Two *Lustres* of years are now expiring, since
the Ministers in *London* of both these perswasions declared their readiness to *Walk together according to the Gospel Rules of Communion of Churches.*   Would all that pretend to the Name of
Presbyterian observe the Articles of that *Union,*
the Congregationals in *New England* would readily give them the Right Hand of Fellowship. Especially if they would practice according to some
Essential Articles therein ; particularly that Article which declares, *that none shall be admitted
to all special Ordinances but such as are not only
free from Scandal in their lives, but persons of visi-*
ble

ble Godliness, making a credible profession of cordial Subjection to Christ. And that Article which says, *We are most willing and ready to give an account of our Church proceedings to each other when desired.* Also that Article wherein they say, *we agree that in order to concord, and in weighty and difficult cases, it is needful and according to the mind of Christ, that the Ministers of several Churches be consulted and advised with about such Matters.* Is not the Embodying into a Church State a weighty matter? Is not the Calling and Ordaining a Minister a *Weighty Matter?* They that shall do such things without advising with Neighbour Churches or Ministers, must think of some other name whereby they may be distinguished. For it is a very vain thing for them to pretend to be either Presbyterian or Congregational: when the *Fundamental Articles of their Union are manifestly* transgressed & violated. For my own part I have many years desired to see an *Union* of these two *Reforming Parties.*

When I was last at *London,* I did that little I was Capable of, to promote that *Union* which ha's been happily Effected. And I account it one of the greatest Mercies of my Life, that ever I was at all instrumental in so Blessed a work. In several points, wherein those of the Congregational perswasion differ from the other, I am satisfyed in my own Judgment, that they have Truth on their side; nevertheless, there have been as Eminent men for Piety & Learning of the Presbyterian perswasion, as any the World ha's in this last Age been Blessed with, whom it is an
affliction

affliction at all to differ from I therefore finifh, with the words of a Great man among us, (z) who fpeaking of fome Presbyterian Divines, thus Expreffeth himfelf, *Thofe Godly Learned Divines we do fo highly Efteem, & fo deeply Reverence in the Lord, that were the caufe our own, & not the Lords, we fhould rather let it fall, than defend it, by Oppofition to the Grave Judgement of fuch Holy Saints.*

(z) Mr. Cotton. *way of the Churches.* p. 84.

THE END.

ERRATA. Page 11 l. 19. for it will r. will it ? p. 17 l 18 r. ennuntiate p. 26 l 21 r. fingula præfentibus p. 40 l 12 r Church p 51 l 4 r. Tigurin p 67 l 4 r. Baptife p 69 l Antipcn r wrefled p 72 l ult r Pol. ecclef p 84 l 9 Laick. definitive p 89 l 27 r Sutliff. p 93 l 27 r Marriages. p 110 l 13 r Literæ p 117 l 9 for practifed profeffed, for the r. our. r

THE CONTENTS.

THE CONTENTS.

THE
DOCTRINE
OF
Instituted Churches
Explained and Proved
FROM THE
WORD
OF
GOD.

By Solomon Stoddard, A. M. *Minister* of the Gospel in
Northampton, New-England.

LONDON:
Printed for *Ralph Smith*, at the Bible under the *Piazza* of the *Royal*
Exchange in Cornhil. 1700.

THE
DOCTRINE
OF
Inftituted CHURCHES

Explained, and Proved from the WORD of GOD.

CHAP. I.

The Word of God gives us fufficient Light, to direct us about Inftituted Churches and all Adminiftrations therein.

THE Nature of an Inftituted Church and the Ordinances to be attended therein, have been matter of great Inquiry in thefe latter Ages. And thofe Inquiries have been Accompanied with great Animofities, Difcords and Perfecutions: Thofe forms and methods that have been admired by fome, have been decryed by others, and Multitudes of People are left at a lofs whether there be any certain Rule to Guide us; or any certainty to be attained in thefe things.

Two things efpecially have hindred thofe that have been ftudious in thefe points, from giving fatisfaction to others : One of them is, that fome of them have been exceeding tenacious of the Traditions and Ancient ufages of the Church, not confidering how difmal a Corruption and Degeneracy did in a little time prevail : whereby it comes to pafs that thofe things are obtruded upon us as Rules, which were the Blemifhes and Errors of the Ancient Church : They have a Veneration for antiquity and adopt the fayings of Ancient

Fathers

Fathers for Canonical. The other is, that some have attempted to compile a compleat Platform, out of the Books of the New Testament alone, looking on all Old Testament Rules, relating to Church Affairs, as out of Date: but if we would have a right understanding of the mind of God in these things, must not be our dependance upon traditions, neither must we confine our selves to one part of Scripture, but search into the whole Word of God impartially.

It is certain that God does fully direct us in the Scripture, concerning the Affairs of his House; as the Word of God doth perfectly direct us how we should behave our selves in the Family and in the Common-wealth, so in the Church: There is no need of any Addition to the Scriptures: There needs an Interpretation of the Word, but nothing at all to be added to it: God doth not give us some broken pieces of a Platform; but hath revealed his whole will in that matter: We are not left under a necessity of missing the Rule or guessing at it. God hath described to us the whole Body of Church Affairs: *For the Scripture is a perfect Rule of Life*, Psal. 19. 7. 2 Tim. 3. 17, 18. *Men shall be blamed for nothing at the Day of Judgment, but what the Scripture does Condemn*, Rev. 20. 12. *What God hath not revealed to us, is no Rule to us: And God hath no where else revealed the Rule but in the Scripture.* As we have no extraordinary Prophets to reveal the mind of God; So there are no unwritten traditions to make known the mind of God in this matter.

There be three sorts of Rules in Scripture to guide us in Church Affairs.　H.

1. *General Moral Rules*: These Rules give us light in many Church Affairs; So that Rule of *Loving God and our Neighbour*, Mat. 22 37, 38, 39. So that Rule of *not partaking in other Mens Sins*, 1 Tim. 5. 22. So that Rule of *Peace and Edification*, Rom. 14. 19, 20. So that Rule of *doing things decently and in order*, 1 Cor. 14. 20. So that Rule, Phil. 4. 8. So that Rule of *Humility*, 1 Pet. 5. 3. These Rules and such like shew us our Duty in many Cases. For,

1. There be many things necessary which there is no Institution about: God was more particular with the Jews, because the Church then was in its Infancy, than he is with us: So we have no institution, how many Elders to have in a Church, how often to Pray or Sing on the Sabbath: *How often to partake of the Lords Supper*, 1 Cor. 11. 26. So there is no particular institution for Moderators in Churches, in case of a vacancy of Elders: About Preaching without ordination: About the Limits and Bounds of particular Churches: There be abundance of other particulars, about Fasts, matters of

Discipline,

Discipline, the Age of Persons to be admitted to the Lords Supper, which are to be determined by Moral Rules.

2. Many things that are commanded in Church Affairs are the proper consequences of *Moral* Rules: And so don't need an institution: There be many things occasionally commanded: Which do not properly belong to Divine institutions, that are not Branches of the second Commandment, but proper deduction from *Moral* Rules; So that about Reconciliation to an offended Brother, *Matth.* 5. 23, 24. *For Christ did not now make new Jewish institutions*: So that about private dealing with an offending Brother, *Matth.* 18. 15, 16. So those Rules, 1 *Tim.* 5. 17, 19. 1 *Cor.* 11. 28. And many others are plain *Moral* Duties.

3. *Moral* Rules must be attended in Church Affairs as well as in other things: Rules for doing things that are for Peace, Edification, and for the good of our Neighbours, bind in Ecclesiastical cases as well as in Civil and Domestical: Therefore they are Generally Propounded, *Phil.* 4. 8. Yea, *there is more weight to be laid on them, then on institutions, Mar.* 12. 33. We must never Act contrary to *Moral* Rules; Churches are bound to *Moral* Rules, as well as other Societies: We have no liberty in the Administration of the things of Gods House to break *Moral* Rules.

2. Old Testament institutions: A great part of Old Testament institutions are abolished: All typical Laws are out of Date: But some institutions that were in force then are in force now: Thus Church Societies, the Preaching of the Word, Fasts, Thanksgivings, are to be attended still. Consider,

1. They and we are under the same Gospel, there was the same way of Salvation then as now, they were under a Covenant of Grace and Saved by Christ as well as we, *Heb.* 4. 2. Hence there be several things common to them and us: Hence the People of God under the Old and New Testament must be such as have a visible Union to Christ; they and we must have signs representing Christ, 1 *Cor.* 10. 3, 4.

2. The Nature of a Church is the same under both Testaments: A Church is not one kind of thing in the Old Testament and another in the New: But it has the same essence and definition: The matter of the Church and the form is the same: The Church then stood in the same relation to God, was appointed for Communion with God, and enjoyed his presence as now.

3. There were several Ordinances in the Jewish Church, that had no particular reference to the times before Christ; or to any particular condition of that People: And such Ordinances seem to be of

B
force

force still, as their, having an holy Convocation, *Lev.* 23. 13. So, much of the work of the Priests, they were to teach the People, *Deut.* 33. 10. They were to bless the People, *Num.* 6. 23. So it was their manner in solemn Prayer and Blessing to lay on hands: So Excomunication, which is to continue in the Christian Church, *Matth.* 18. 17.

4. We are referred in some cases to those institutions: God sends us to the Law for light, directs us to do as was appointed in the Old Testament: So about Womens not speaking in the Church, 1 *Cor.* 14. 34. So about the maintenance of Ministers, *Gal.* 6. 6. 1 *Cor.* 9. 13, 14.

3. New Testament institutions, there were some institutions appointed by Christ under the Gospel, these are few; principally, what Officers shall be in the Church, *The Sacraments of Baptism, and the Lords Supper, and the first day Sabbath.*

1. We must distinguish between Temporal and Perpetual institutions: Some institutions were only for a time, as the Office of the Apostles: *So the anointing of the sick with Oyl, Jam.* 5.14. There are others that are to continue to the end of the World: *So is Baptism,* Matth. 20. *The Lords Supper,* 1 Cor. 11. 26. These Ordinances will not be removed as *Jewish* Ceremonies; *Heb.* 13. 28.

2. Distinguish between approved practises and institutions, there were many practises and institutions, there were many practises in the primitive times that were approved, yet not binding to us: The Church at *Jerusalem* had seven Deacons, *Acts* 6. 5. *They did Baptize in private Houses,* Act. 10. 33. *Christ sent out his Disciples two and two,* Luk. 10. 1. This doth not shew that these things were institutions ; that is meet to be done in one case, that is not meet to be done in another: One or two Examples shew the Lawfulness of a practise, but do not make it a binding Rule.

CHAP.

CHAP. II.

The Nature of Instituted Churches Explained.

THE Word *Church* is used Equivocally, there are three senses especially, wherein it is used in the Scripture.

First, It is taken for those that are Spiritually United unto Christ, the mistical Body of Christ, *Eph.* 5. 27. *That he might present it to himself a Glorious Church.*

Secondly, For that part of the World that doth profess the true faith for them that are visible Christians, 1 *Cor.* 15. 9. *I persecuted the Church of God.*

Thirdly, It is taken for an Instituted Church ; this Church is invested by Christ with Spiritual Power and is thus defined : A Church is a Society of Saints joyned together, according to the appointment of Christ for the constant carrying on of his publick Worship : A Church is a Society, a single Person is not a Church, a Church is a Collection or Congregative Body, consisting of many Members, 1 *Cor.* 12. 27. Ye are the Body of Christ and Members in particulars, hence it is compared to a flock and other Collective Bodies : It is a Society of Saints, *The Members of a Church are Saints by calling*, 1 Cor. 11. 12. To the Church of God which is at *Corinth*, to them, which are sanctified in Christ Jesus, called to be Saints, 1 *Cor.* 14. 33. *In all the Churches of the Saints, the Church of the* Jews *was a Society of Saints*, Psal. 79. 12, 11. Psal. 1. *None are to be Members of Instituted Churches, but those that are Members of the Catholick Church.* Particular Churches are but parts and branches of the Catholick Church, they are the Churches of God, the Body of Christ, the Temple of God, therefore must be Holy. *Therefore Societies of Papists are abusively called Churches* : A Church doth joyn together for the Publick carrying on of the Worship of God : A Family joyning together for the private carrying on of the Worship of God is not a Church ; we read of a Church in the House of *Aquila*, *Rom.* 16. 5. And in the House of *Nymphas*, *Col.* 4. 15. Because there the publick Worship of God was attended : The Church doth joyn for the carrying on of publick Worship ; as the Preaching of the word, the Administration of Sacraments and dispensing of Censures in a publick way.

A Church doth joyn together for the conſtant carrying on of the publick Worſhip of God, for a Church is a Body Corporate, which may continue from Generation to Generation, it is not any occaſional Meeting together, that gives being to a Church : A Church is a ſtanding Society, not depending on any oceaſional Meeting; Therefore a Congregation that meet together on a Lecture Day, from ſeveral Towns to hear the Word Preached are not a Church, neither have any Eccleſiaſtical Power : Yea, a ſynod that meet now and then occaſionally, though it may be called a repreſentative Church, is not a Church properly ; the Members thereof are choſen for a particular occaſion : A Church doth joyn together according to Chriſts appointment ; Chriſt has given a Rule according to which they ought to joyn together, and if Men joyn in Worſhiping with a Church irregularly, that does not make them to be Members of that Church : If a man that lives in one Town where there is a Church, doth joyn conſtantly in worſhiping with another Church, that doth not make him a Member of that Church.

Queſt. *VVho are viſible Saints ?*

Anſw. This Queſtion hath been matter of great debate, and an occaſion of great contention in the Church ; we may not count thoſe only to be Saints, who after the ſtricteſt Examination, give conſiderable evidence that they are Saints : We have no ſuch Rule, the practice of the Apoſtles in admitting Members into the Chriſtian Church, doth not Countenance any ſuch Opinion, neither are we to make Baptized Perſons and Viſible Saints to be the ſame ; for Perſons muſt be Viſible Saints before they are Baptized ; and ſome that are Baptized, may ceaſe to be Viſible Saints ; neither are they only Viſible Saints, that make a profeſſion of the true Religion joyned with an Holy Converſation : Some Men may behave themſelves ſo as to deſerve a ſentence of Excommunication, and yet be Viſible Saints : Viſible Saintſhip and real Saintſhip, may conſiſt with a great deal of iniquity in the Converſation for a time.

Viſible Saints are ſuch as make a ſerious profeſſion of the true Religion, together with thoſe that do deſcend from them, till rejected of God.

1. Such as do make a ſerious profeſſion of the true Religion, are Viſible Saints ; we find the Apoſtles did really accept of ſuch, not waiting to ſee, what their Converſation would be, *Act.* 16, 14, 15. So did *John,* Luk. 7. 29, 30. *Such are to be accepted without delay.*

2. Their Infant Seed are likewiſe Viſible Saints, God gives that Teſtimony for them, 1 *Cor.* 7. 14.

1. Such

3. Such also as descend from them, from Generation to Generation, untill they are rejected by God are Visible Saints; for they that are Visible Saints don't cease to be so, till God hath cast them off; So it was with the Posterity of *Abraham*, if they should carry it wickedly, or if they should fall into Heresy, yet they are Visible Saints, till God hath rejected them; and there are two ways whereby God may shew his rejection of them: One is when they do depart from the Churches of God to Heathen or Antichristian Societies, the other is, when the People that they belong unto and they with them are unchurched by God.

CHAP. III.

Of the Nature of a Congregational Church.

AS a Civil Society doth consist of one Town, or more Towns, so an instituted Church is either Congregational, or that which consists of Divers Congregations.

A Congregational Church is a Church that is bound by the appointment of God to assemble together in one place, in a constant way for the Celebration of his Publick Worship: A Congregational Church, is a Church consisting of one Congregation: Such we read of, *Act.* 20. 7. 1 *Cor.* 14. 23. The form of a Congregational Church is, that they are bound by the appointment of God to assemble in one place in a constant way for the Celebration of his Publick Worship. Some have thought that the form of a Congregational Church is a Church Covenant, explicite or implicite, wherein they bind themselves to walk together according to the order of the Gospel: It is thought that the Children of *Israels* Covenanting with God is a Foundation for this, whereas that Covenant of theirs is no other, then what all Christians do make, when they make a profession of Faith and Obedience; we never read of any particular Covenant made in the Synagogues, which Answer to our Congregations, whereby the Members of one Synagogue were bound one to another. It is pleaded that nothing else can bind a free People one to another but an Ecclesiastical Covenant; but there is some what else that binds a free People in the same Town to mutual subjection, to the Government of the Town; and tho Christians are a free People, yet they have not a Licentious Liberty but are bound

C

by

by God, and likewise by their own profession to the Rule of the Gospel : Neither is there any necessity of such a bond to distinguish one Church from another, and to avoid confusion of Churches, we read of no such particular Covenant in the New Testament, we have no precept for it, we have no president for it ; we read of many Congregational Churches, but there is no Syllable in the Word of God, intimating any such thing, neither is there any need of it.

The Members of a Congregation are bound to carry on the Worship together, this is Gods appointment, that his People that live together should carry on his Worship together, the Christians at *Corinth* are the Church of *Corinth*, 1 Cor. 1. 2. And the Christians at *Ephesus* are the Church of *Ephesus* ; Order calls for it, that where Men live, there they joyn together to carry on the Work of Christ. If a Christian live in a Town, where there is a Church, he is immediately bound to joyn with that Church ; and that Church is bound to him to govern him, and give him Christian Priviledges ; there be some cases wherein there is need of humane prudence in determining how many Churches shall be in some Towns : Some. Towns arise to be numerous, so that it is fit they should be joyned in several Societies : And some are so small and lye so near together, that it is fit that two or more should make one Church, in such cases God has appointed that the bounds of Churches be set either by General agreement, or by order from Authority, but there is no occasion that every Member should Covenant particularly with the Church : Grant this particular Covenant to be the form of a Church, and then a Christian may continue a considerable time, without any relation to a particular Church, tho he lives where there is a Church : And then a Man may be a Member of the Church of *Corinth* for seven years together, and live all that while in Communion with the Church at *Jerusalem* ; a Covenant which he lives in the continual breach of, makes a Member at *Corinth*, and according to some, gives him a right to all Ordinances : Grant this particular Covenant and we shall be to seek, what Church many Children do belong to, the father is in Covenant with one Church, the Mother with another, the Child was Baptized in a third and lives in a fourth : This Doctrine of the particular Covenant which is wholly unscriptural, is the reason that many among us are shut out of the Church, to whom Church Priviledges do belong.

C H A P.

CHAP. IV

Of the Priviledges of Congregational Churches:

THE great Priviledge of Congregational Churches is to choose their own Officers, they have a liberty given to them by God to choose suteable Persons to Office, they are limited to Persons fitly qualified, but the Priviledge of choosing them doth belong unto the Church, it is very probable, that the Synagogues of the *Jews* had liberty to choose their own Ministers ; if they were confined to the Tribe of *Levi*, yet out of the Levites they choose for themselves ; However, thus it ought to be in Christian Churches, the Apostles ordered the Church of *Jerusalem* to choose their own Deacons, *Act*. 6. 3, 4. They did not take upon them to prescribe, who the Persons should be, and impose Deacons on them, but referred the matter to their own choice; and the People nominated two, out of which God chose one to be an Apostle, *Act*. 1. 23.

Besides, it is the Priviledge of all free Societies to choose their own Officers ; such Countrys as are conquer'd don't chuse their own Rulers, nor such Countrys where the Government is Hereditary, but such as are free, neither under the Power of Conquerors, nor the Bond of a Covenant do choose their own Officers either mediately or immediately : All the Power that Men have over a free People is by their own consent, directly or indirectly, excepting such cases wherein God is pleased to appoint Rulers, or some who shall appoint Rulers over them ; God appointed *Aaron* and his Posterity to the Office of the Priesthood in *Israel*, but God hath not appointed any Officers in Churches now, neither hath he appointed any that shall impose Officers over them, but hath left them to their free choice.

Yea, where a Church hath teaching, or Ruling Elders, or both, there is no necessity that they should consent to the choice, if they do not consent, yet if there be the consent of the Major part, the choice is vallid ; the Officers ought to submit thereto, unless they have some weighty Objection, the Act of the Major part, is the Act of the Community, that which is the Priviledge of the Community, must

must not be wrested out of their hands; It is beyond the Power of the Officers to disanul their Act.

And as the Church hath Power to choose their own Officers, so in case of need they have Power to choose those that shall supply the want of Officers for a time, the Church is entrusted with sufficient Power in order to the carrying on of Gods work: Therefore in case of the vacancy of a Pastor, they may choose one to Preach to them for a time, in case they have no Elders, they may choose a Moderator; In case they have no Deacons they may choose one to do the Deacons work, yea in case there be need, they may choose some other Minister of the Gospel, to Administer the Seals of the Covenant, or perform some Act of Government upon a particular occasion.

By the same reason that a Church may choose its own Officers, it may also choose its own Servants; *Phebe* is called a Servant of the Church, *Rom.* 6. 2. So were Widdows, for they were not ordained; So their Sexton and such as shall over-see the Buildings, or any other Servants that may be for the conveniency of the Church. This Church Priviledge of choosing Officers, doth only belong to the Brethren of the Church, the Brethren are said to choose the Deacons, *Act.* 6: 3. *And Women have not Power in this matter*, 1 Cor. 14. 33. *Let your Women keep silence in the Churches*, 1 Tim. 2. 12. Suffer not a Woman to teach, nor to usurp Authority over the Man, it is inconsistent with that State of subjection which God hath put them into, if they might vote, they might over-rule the Men, and by the same Rule, those Males that are not their own Masters, (as Children that are not at their own dispose, and Servants) have nothing to do to vote in the Church they that are not free, are not to partake of this Liberty.

CHAP. V.

Of the Officers of Congregational Churches and their Power.

THE Officers of Congregational Churches are either Elders or Deacons, the Elders are either teaching Elders, or Ruling Elders. The work of the Teaching Elders lies principally in these five

five things; they are to be the mouth of the People to God, both in the publick Assembly, and privately in case of sickness, they are to Preach the Word of God, they are to Administer the Seals of the Covenant, they together with the Ruling Elders, are to Govern the Church, and they are to bless the People.

Such Learned Men as are suteably qualified, but not in Office may upon occasion discharge some part of this work ; but there are some other parts of it, that they may not meddle with, those Acts which are Acts of Natural Worship may be performed by them, as praying and Preaching; but such Ministerial Acts as do depend wholly upon institution, they may not perform, as the Administration of Sacraments, the dispencing of Censures and an Authoritative blessing ; these are performed only by Virtue of an Institution, therefore are to be done only according to an Institution.

A teaching Elder by Virtue of his relation to a particular Church, is bound to attend his work in that Church: And by Virtue of that relation, he has no Authority to perform Acts of Office to any other Church, or to the Members of any other Church. Assembling with his own Church : Pastoral Power over a particular Church gives him no Power over any that are of that Church, his relation to them gives him no Power over any other.

But every Man that is a Pastor of a particular Church stands in a more General relation, as a Minister of Christ; some that are not Pastors to particular Congregations are yet Ministers of Christ; and every Man that is a Pastor to a particular Church is a Minister of Christ, and by Virtue of that Relation he may do Acts of Office to the Members of other Churches occasionally assembling with his own, and towards other Churches being desired, when he can conveniently be spared from his own, and towards particular Persons that are Members of no Church.

The Levites were the Ministers of God before they had Relation to any particular Synagogue ; *Paul* hath Office Power over the Brethren as well as the Church of God, *Act.* 26. 17, 18. The Church at *Jerusalem* sent *Barabas* to *Antiock*, to officiate as a Minister, *Act.* 11. And they that have Authority to Preach have also to Baptize, *Mat.* 28. 19, 20. We find that *Paul* did not Baptize such as he brought over to the Christian faith, but committed that work to some other inferiour Ministers that were in Company with him, 1 *Cor.* 1. 14. And this he did after the Example of Christ, *John* 4. 2. There is need that some have Office-Power now to Preach to the Heathens, as well as there was in the Days of the Apostles, and

there

there may be several now that Baptism doth belong to ; as well as *Cornelius*, the Eunuch and the Jailor and others, therefore there are some appointed by God for that Service.

The Teaching Officer is appointed by Christ to Baptize and Adminiſter the Lords Supper, and therefore he is made the Judge by God, what Perſons thoſe ordinances are to be Adminiſtred to, and it is not the work either of the Brethren or Ruling Elders, any ways to intermeddle in that Affair or Limit him ; we never read that the Apoſtles did adviſe with the Church, whether they ſhould Baptize ſuch as offered themſelves. As the Adminiſtration of theſe ordinances is committed to them, ſo the Judging concerning thoſe who they are to be Adminiſtred unto, as they are to Judge what ſubject to teach upon, and as the Deacon is to Judge who is to be relieved ; So the Miniſter is to Judge who is to be Baptized and Admitted to the Lords Supper. The Ruling Elders are to joyn with the Teaching Elders in Rule and Government ; theſe Officers are called Governments, 1 *Cor.* 12. Such as Rule, *Rom.* 12. Diſtinguiſhed from ſuch as Labour in the Word and Doctrine, 1 *Tim.* 5. The Teaching Elders with the Ruling Elders, make the Presbytery of the Church ; with whom the Government of the Church is entruſted : The Power of Cenſuring offenders in the Church, and abſolving of Penitents, doth belong alone to theſe, the Brethren of the Church are not to intermeddle with it. The Elders are to Rule over the Church, and therefore not to be over-ruled by the Brethren, it is the work of the Elders to rule well, 1 *Tim.* 5. 17. The Members of the Church are to be obedient to the Elders, therefore not to controul them in their Government, *Heb.* 12. 17. The Elders of the ꟾewiſh Church, had the Power of Government of the Church in their hands, hence we read of the Rulers and Chief Rulers of the Synagogues, *Act.* 18. *Deut.* 21. 5. The Elders have the Keys of the Kingdom of Heaven committed to them, *Matth.* 16. 18. The meaning is, that he ſhould be an Elder and Ruler of the Church, it is ſpoken of as a Perſonal reward of his profeſſion.

Obj. *Matth.* 18. 17. *Tell it to the Church, this* *implies the Power of the Brethren.*

Anſw. 1. By the Church is meant the Eccleſiaſtical Authority in diſtinction from the Civil.

2. It is not harſh by the Church to intend the Elders of the Church. See, *Numb.* 24. 25.

3. By the Church muſt be meant the Elders of the Church ; for this was a Rule in the Day when it was ſpoken, and there was

now

now no Church in Being, but the *Jewish* Church ; in which all the Power of Government was with the Elders.

Obj. 1 *Cor.* 5. 1, 4. *The Church was ordered to caſt out the Inceſtu- ous Perſon, and* 2 *Cor.* 12. *His Puniſhment is ſaid to be inflicted by many.*

Anſw. 1. They may be only required to publiſh a ſentence of Ex- communication from *Paul.*

2. It is common in Scripture, to attribute that which is done by the Ruler to the Publick Society ; as when God requires that the People of *Judah* do Acts of Publick Juſtice, he doth not intend that the People ſhould intrude into that work, but that the Ruler do it,

3. Whereas it is ſaid that the Puniſhment was inflicted by many, it may be read before many ; Deacons were choſen at firſt to have an over-ſight of the Poor, *Act.* 6. And there is nothing plainly de- clared to be their work beſides that. It is intimated, *Rom.* 12. 8. That it is their work to ſhew mercy and to give ; It is Generally put upon them to take care about the Miniſters dues, and about the Proviſion for the Lords Table, which is gathered from that phraſe, *Act.* 6. 2. It is not meet that we ſhould leave the Word of God and ſerve Tables, but there ſeems to be no neceſſity, that there muſt be a Church Officer to do ; all that work which the Church is to ſee done ; ſome things may be done by Servants.

CHAP. VI.

Of the Ordination of Church Officers.

THere are none to be ordained Officers in the Church of God, but thoſe that have a regular call to thoſe Offices ; Ordinati- on is the Admiſſion of Perſons into their Office, or the conſumma- tion of their call, needful to the regular Execution of their Office ; it includes in it firſt, a ſolemn imploring of the preſence of God with them in their Office.

Two things are requiſite unto a call ; One is, the approbation or invitation of thoſe whom God hath entruſted with that care ; the other is, the conſent of the Perſon invited ; the former may be a call to the latter, and bind the Perſon to accept, but there muſt be

both

both, before he is called of God to enter immediately upon the work of the Office ; before he be accepted of God as an Officer.

The work of the Deacon being confined to one Congregation, the invitation of that Church, is sufficient without any further approbation, *Act.* 6. 7.

God having appointed all his Holy Ordinances to be Administred in a particular Church ; in case of necessity, the choice of a Church is sufficient (without any further approbation) unto the calling of Elders, as when *Luther* and others broke off from Popery.

Yet Elders having not only Power over their particular Churches, but also over others, and God having committed to National and Provincial Churches, the care of particular Congregations, it is requisite, when it may be obtained, that there be an approbation of Men chosen to be Elders, by some deputed by the National or Provincial Church.

Furthermore, some Persons being to be entrusted with the Office of being Ministers of Christ, who have no call to any particular Congregation, there is need that they have the approbation of some deputed by the Church in that Country, or at least by a particular Congregation : The Persons that are to perform this Act of Ordination, ought to be such as are most suitable to the Ends of Ordination, *viz.* The signifying approbation and the obtaining the presence of God with him ; sometimes we find that extraordinary Persons have ordained a Person to extraordinary Office, 2 *Tim.* 1. 6. Sometimes we find that extraordinary Persons have ordained ordinary Officers, *Act.* 14. 23. And there is command given to extraordinary Officers to ordain ordinary, 1 *Tim.* 5. 22. 1 *Tit.* 5. Sometimes we find that extraordinary Officers, and ordinary have joyned in the ordaining of extraordinary ; *Act.* 13. 1, 5. Sometimes we find that ordinary Officers, have ordained an extraordinary Officer ; 1 *Tim.* 4. 14. In a Provincial Church that is in order, Ministers ought to be ordained by such Elders, as are appointed by the Publick Ecclesiastical Authority of the Land.

In such Countrys where the Church is not in order, it is meet that the Ministers be ordained by some suiteable Persons deputed by the Neighbouring Elders, but in case of necessity, Ministers may be ordained by some of the Brethren appointed by the Church to that service.

The Ordination of Deacons ought to be performed by Elders of the same Church, in case there be any, or by the Brethren in case there be none.

A

A Minister removing from one Church to another, may be ordained a second time, as *Paul* was, and probably *Timothy*.

It is the manner in some places to give to Churches at their Constitution, and to Ministers at their Ordination, the right hand of fellowship, from the Example of the Apostles; but it may be doubted whether that was any more then a civil Act, if it be an Institution, we are to seek whether it be to be done to all those Persons, that we have fellowship with, and when it ought to be performed.

CHAP. VII.

Of the *Worship* that is to be attended in Congregational Churches.

THE End of this Constitution of Congregational Churches is the joynt Celebration of the Worship of God, herein hey differ from civil Societies, that meet together for the management of civil affairs.

The first part of Worship that is to be attended in the Church of God is Prayer; Prayer which includes in it, besides Petitions, confessions and thankfgivings, is a principal part of Gods Worship, Prayer is a part of Gods Worship, *Pfal.* 107. 32. *Pfal.* 149. 1. This is to be attended in the Church, *Act.* 1. 14. *Act.* 4. 24. *Act.* 6. 4. These publick Prayers are to be ordinarily performed by the Teaching Elders; in case there be a Vacancy it may be performed by the Ruling Elders, or some of the Brethren, but ordinarily the Minister is to be the mouth of the People to God, *Act.* 6. 4.

These publick Prayers ought not to be made by the reading of prescribed forms of Prayer, out of a Book, he that hath not the gift of Prayer, is not fit to be a Minister; there may be some exempt Cases wherein it is Lawful for a Man to Pray in a form which they have Learned out of a Book, but the imposing of such a thing on Men is an addition to Divine Institutions, and the ordinary practising of it is of very bad Consequence; it quenches and stifles the Spirit of Prayer, indulges Men in Idleness and is very unprofitable to others.

E

The

The second part of Worship to be performed in the Church, is Singing of Pſalms ; this is a Moral Duty not belonging peculiarly to the time of the Old Teſtament, as Chriſt with his Diſciples did pra-ctiſe it ; So afterwards *Paul* and *Silas*, *Act.* 16. And we have poſitive commands for it, *Eph.* 5. 16. *Col.* 3. 16. *Jam.* 5. 13. In the primitive times when God gave to all extraordinary Gifts of his Spirit.

It was the manner ſometimes for one Man to ſing a *Pſalm*, and the Congregation to ſay *Amen*, 1 *Cor.* 14. 15, 16. But now it is moſt proper for us to joyn together in Singing of *Pſalms*, as Chriſt and his Diſciples did, and as *Moſes* and the Children of *Iſrael* did, *Exod.* 15. 1.

As the Church of *Iſrael* were wont to Sing the *Pſalms* of *David*, ſo (tho we are not forbidden to Sing *Pſalms* of a private compo-ſure) it is Lawful for us to Sing the *Pſalms* of *David* and other Scripture *Pſalms*, the Apoſtle when he directs us to Sing *Pſalms*, *Hymns* and Spiritual Songs, E*ph. Col.* 3. Hath a manifeſt reſpect to the diviſion of *Davids Pſalms*, ſome things in thoſe *Pſalms* are not ſo ſuteable to our preſent Caſe, ſo it is in what we read, yet thoſe *Pſalms* are very ſuteable for us to meditate upon ; and contain in them much Inſtruction and Incouragement, and becauſe they were indicted by the Spirit of God, are more proper to affect our hearts and excite the workings of Grace, then ſuch as are of a private Compoſure.

A third part of Worſhip is the Preaching and Teaching of the Word ; the Preaching of the Word is to be attended to the End of the World, *Matth.* 28. 19. 20. It is the Duty of Miniſters to Preach the Word, 2 *Tim.* 4. 2. A Miniſter is called a Preacher, *Rom.* 12. 14. This is a ſpecial means to advance the Converſion of Sinners and Edification of Saints.

Altho it be the ſpecial Office and Duty of Teaching Elders, and ordained Miniſters of the Goſpel, yet Preaching being a Moral Du-ty, it is lawful for thoſe, who are not ordained Miniſters, to Preach the Goſpel ; Yea, in ſome caſes it is Lawful for ſuch Men who are not devoted to the Miniſtry, provided they have ſuteable abilities.

The reading of large Portions of Scripture upon the Sabbath Day, which was conſtantly Practiſed by the *Jewiſh* Church, is not ſo particularly now required by God, there was great need of it in thoſe Ages, when the World had not the benefit of Preaching ; but there is no inſtitution requiring any ſuch ſer-
vice

vice of us, any further then the Rule of Edification calls for it.

Minifters are not bound to obferve any particular method in their Preaching, they may Preach either by expounding fome Portion of Scripture, or by raifing a Doctrine from a particular Text, and applying of it, or by explaining of a Catechifm, or in any other profitable way. Minifters have Power to Catechife their hearers, not only that they may know their fitnefs to participate at the Lords Table, but alfo in order to their growth in knowledge tho it may be prefumed that many Perfons are inquifitive and ftudious, yet there are many others who are not to be confided in, and the Minifter hath Power by Virtue of his Paftoral charge, to fee that they Learn; reafon dictates this to be a moft futeable method, as in the Learning of Arts and Languages, fo in the Learning of the way of falvation, the moft proper and profitable ways of teaching, are to be ufed by Minifters.

A fourth part of Worfhip is Baptifm; this is an ordinance appointed by Chrift himfelf to be a perpetual Ordinance in the Chriftian Church, It was publifhed by *John* before, by Virtue of an Inftitution, but afterwards declared by Chrift, to be a ftanding ordinance in the Church.

It is very likely that the form afterwards ufed by *John* and his Difciples was, that they did Baptize in the Name of the Lord Jefus, *Act.* 19. 5. But feeing Chrift did exprefly command his Apoftles before his affention, to *Baptize in the Name of the Father, Son, and Holy Ghoft*, we have no reafon to think that the firft Teachers of the Gofpel did ufe any other form, and when we read that the *Samaritans, were Baptized in the Name of the Lord Jefus, Act.* 8. 18. And that *Peter* ordered that *Cornelius* and his Company fhould be Baptized in the Name of the Lord, *Act.* 10. 48. No more feems to be intended by it, then their being Baptized according to the inftitution of the Lord Jefus.

The Perfons that are fent to Adminifter Baptifm, are the fame that are fent to Preach the Word, *Matth.* 28. 19, 20. Tho the Apoftles did fometimes decline it, yet we have reafon to conclude that they committed it to Inferiour Minifters; After the Example of Chrift, who did not commit it to the People, but to his Difciples, *John* 4. 2. Therefore fuch Preachers as are not ordained Minifters, are not to Baptize.

Baptism may be Administred either in the Publick Assembly or in private, there is no appointment that necessitates the publick performance of it, there is nothing in the Nature of the ordinance that doth necessitate it; and we find that the Apostles and Apostolical Men, did it as there was occasion, both publickly and privately, *Act.* 8. 38. and 9. 18. and 16. 33.

There is no necessity that Persons be Members of any particular Congregation before they be Baptized; Persons before they be Members of any particular Congregation, may have that qualification that gives them a right to Baptism, *viz.* Visible Saintship; many that were Baptized in the first times did not belong to any particular Congregation of Christians, and tho many of them did belong to particular *Jewish* Congregations or Synagogues, yet some did not, *Act.* 16. 33.

Such adult Persons as make such a profession of the Christian Faith, as is Morally sincere, are to be Baptized; as doth appear by the Example of *John*, Christ himself, *Phillip* and others, who were directed by the Spirit of God; and none were refused that did seriously tender themselves to be Baptized.

Such Infants as are descended from the Covenant People of God by either Parent, are to be Baptized, 1 *Cor.* 7. 14. Such Infants as do descend from Parents that are under Church censures, for immoralities, are not to be denied Baptism, because Excommunication doth not cut Men off from the Covenant of God; such Infants as are the Children of Heathens, belonging to the Families of the People of God, are Incorporated into the Covenant and are to be Baptized; when the Apostle saith, 1 *Cor.* 7. 14. Else were your Children unclean, he speaks of them as they come into the World; yet it follows not, but when they are taken into the Families of Christians, they do become Holy; such were to be Circumcised under the Law.

A fifth part of Worship is the Lords Supper; which was instituted by Christ a little before his Death, to be a standing Ordinance in the Christian Church; all such Professors of the Christian Faith, as are of blameless Conversation, and have knowledge to examine themselves and discern the Lords Body, are to be admitted to the Lords Supper.

Three things are requisite in order to admission to the Lords Supper; First, Visible Saintship, and that is found in such Persons; all professors walking blamelesly are Visible Saints; the *Members* of the *Jewish* Church are often called Saints in the Scripture, who did
give

give no further evidence of their Saintſhip, a Profeſſion of the faith joyned with a good Converſation, is a ſufficient ground for Charity, theſe ·are marks that we are directed in the Scripture to Judge of *Mens* Saintſhip by ; The Apoſtle did accept of ſuch Perſons for Viſible Saints, *Men* that have theſe Characters, are not viſibly wicked, therefore they are Viſible Saints ; theſe properties are the proper Fruits of Saintſhip, and therefore conſtitute *Men* Viſible Saints; ſuch a profeſſion as being ſincere makes a *Man* a real Saint, being *Morally* ſincere, makes a *Man* a Viſible Saint. That whereby Godly *Men* do make their Saintſhip Viſible, does make *Men* Viſible Saints, *viz.* A profeſſion of the truth and a good Converſation.

A ſecond requiſite is, that they be not ſcandalous ; a *Man* that is really and viſibly Godly may fall into a ſcandal, and upon that account be forbidden to participate at the Lords Table, but when their Converſation is good, they cannot be hindred upon that Account.

A third requiſite is, that they have knowledge to examine themſelves and diſcern the Lords Body ; for the want of this Infants are denied the Lords Supper.

Thoſe Adult Perſons that are fit to be admitted into the Church, are to be admitted to the Lords Supper.

All Adult Perſons that are fit to be admitted into the Church, ordinarily have all thoſe qualifications requiſite to the participation of the Lords Supper.

They make profeſſion of the true Faith and are of good Converſation, they have knowledge of the principles of Religion, and ſo are able to examine themſelves, and if any of them ſhould not underſtand the Nature of that ordinance, they may ſoon be ſufficiently informed.

Two things are evident in the practiſe of the Apoſtles, one is, that they readily admitted ſuch into the Church, as made a profeſſion of the Chriſtian Faith, *Act.* 2. *Act.* 6. We never read that ever they denied Admiſſion to any Man or Woman that made that profeſſion ; the other is, that all that were thus received by them, were admitted to the Lords Supper, 1 *Cor.* 10. 17. *Act.* 2. 24. They made no diſtinction of the Adult Members of the Church, into Communicants and Non-Communicants.

Thoſe that are commanded by God to participate of the Lords Supper, are to be admitted to the Lords Supper, but all profeſſors that have a good Converſation and Knowledge are commanded by God to participate in the Lords Supper; if Men have not theſe Qua-

F   lifications

lifications they are not obliged immediately to participate in the Lords Supper, for it would be a sin if they should: But having these Qualifications they are bound, provided they have opportunity. Christ has laid this Law upon Professors, 1 *Cor.* 11. 24, 25. The persons here commanded are not only true Believers, then none can do it with a good Conscience but those that know themselves to be true Believers; then the Church Authority can require none but true Believers to come, the Persons therefore required to partake are such professors as carry it inoffensively, and if such are bound to come, the Church is bound to receive them, they may not hinder any Man from doing his Duty.

There can be no just cause assigned, why such Men should be debarred from coming to the Lords Supper, they are not to be debarred for not giving the highest evidence of sincerity; There never was any such Law in the Church of God, that any should be debarred Church Priviledges because they did not give the highest evidence of sincerity, nor for want of the Exercise of Faith; it is unreasonable to believe Men to be visible Saints from their Infancy till they be forty or fifty years of Age, and yet not capable of coming to the Lords Supper, for want of the Exercise of Faith; they are not to be denied because of the weakness of Grace, they that have the least Grace need to have it Nourished and Cherished.

Such Adult Persons as are worthy to be admitted into the Church, or being in the Church are worthy to be continued without censure, are to be admitted to the Lords Supper; it is utterly unreasonable to deny the Adult Members of the Church, the Lords Supper, and yet not lay them under censure; If they are guilty of any such offence as to be denyed the Lords Supper, why are they not censured? If they are not worthy to be censured, why are they kept from the Lords Supper?

There are some Scriptures that have been thought to hold forth a need of somewhat further, in order to participation in the Lords Supper, which if they be examined will be found to be strained beyond the Import of them, *Psal.* 6. 16. *David* saith, I will tell you what the Lord hath done for my Soul, hence it is argued, that Men should give an Account of the manner of their Conversion, in order to their Admission; but if it should be granted that *David* doth respect the work of Regeneration, doth it follow because he was willing to talk of it, that they might make a Law to bind him to do it in the Synagogue, or doth it follow that *David* offered to do it in order to his joyning with the *Jewish* Church, *Act.* 2. 37. They
were

were pricked at the heart, before they were admitted into the Church, but let it be confidered that many others were joyned to the Chriftian Church, of whom we read no fuch thing, and here is no living Rule that others muft declare that they are pricked at the heart before their Admiffion ; yea it is certain, that thefe did not declare their trouble, in order to their Admiffion into the Church, but in order to their Direction ; yea, it doth not appear that thefe Men were under a work of Converfion at this time, they might be Godly Men before, the thing that ftung them was a National fin, which in probability, they had no hand in ; For the greater part of them, were ftrangers, come up to keep the Feaft of *Pentecoft*, and were greatly affected with the fin which the Nation of the *Jews* were guilty of in Crucifying of Chrift, *Act.* 9. 26, 27. The Church at *Jerufalem* refufed to admit *Paul* to their Communion, till they were informed by *Barnabas*, of his Converfion; but it doth not appear that *Paul* did then defire to participate with them in the Lords Supper, poffibly it might be only in hearir ; of the Word and Prayer, and the reafon why they were unwilling to receive him, was not any doubt whether his Converfion was fincere, but whether he was a Chriftian ; As if in a Popifh Country, one who had been a violent Perfecutor fhould Effay to joyn himfelf to a Proteftant Congregation, it would be no wonder if they fhould be affraid of him, until they were informed that he was become a Proteftant ; this is no foundation to require of all that joyn to the Church, an Account about the manner of their Converfion. 1 *Pet.* 3. 15. Men are required to be ready to give an Anfwer to every one that asketh them a reafon of the hope that is in them ; but here by the reafon of the hope that is in them, we are not to underftand their experiences of the Grace of God, but the grounds of their Faith, the reafon why they did believe the Chriftian Doctrine? This is evident, becaufe he is fpeaking of Perfecution, *v.* 14. and becaufe he directs them to give their Anfwer with meeknefs and fear.

Queft: *Here it may be enquired, whether fuch Perfons as have a good Converfation and a Competent Knowledge, may come to the Lords Supper, with a good Confcience, in cafe they know themfelves to be in a Natural Condition?*

Anfw. They may and ought to come, tho they know themfelves to be in a Natural Condition ; this Ordinance is inftituted for all the Adult Members of the Church who are not fcandalous, and therefore muft be attended by them ; as no Man may neglect Prayer, or hearing the Word, becaufe he cannot do it in Faith, fo he may not neglect the Lords Supper.
                                                                    The

The Lords Supper is Inftituted to be a means of Regeneration, it is not appointed for the Converting of Men to the Chriftian Religion, for only fuch as are Converted may partake of it ; but it is not only for the ftrengthening of Saints, but a means alfo to work faving Regeneration.

There be many, according to the Ordinance of Chrift, to be admitted to the Lords Supper, who are not Regenerate, *Matth.* 25. 1, 2. The Kingdom of Heaven is like ten Virgins, five of them were Wife, and five Foolifh, and it can have no other immediate end refpecting thefe, but their Converfion ; the end of all Ordinances is falvation, and therefore to thefe Men it muft be Regeneration, for without it, they cannot be faved.

This Ordinance hath a proper tendency to draw finners to Chrift; in this Ordinance there is a particular Invitation to finners, to come to Chrift for Pardon, here is an affecting Reprefentation of the Virtue of Chrifts fufferings, here is a Seal whereby the Truth of the Gofpel is confirmed, all which are very proper to draw finners to Chrift.

If the Lords Supper be only for the ftrengthening of Saints, then they who are not Saints do profane the Ordinance, when they do partake, and it is not Lawful for them to partake, and then they that do not know themfelves to be Saints, don't know that it is Lawful for them to partake, and fo far as any Man hath fcruples about his Saintfhip, he muft proportionably have fcruples about the Lawfulnefs of his Participation, and fo Sacrament Days which fhould be Days of Comfort, will become Days of Torment.

All other Ordinances are appointed for Regeneration, Prayer, hearing the Word, Baptifm ; fo likewife the cenfures are, that the Soul may be faved in the Day of the Lord Jefus ; they are to further Mens Regeneration, in cafe they be not Converted already, and it would be ftrange if the Lords Supper alone fhould not be appointed for that end, whereas it hath a proper tendency thereunto, and many that come to that Ordinance by the appointment of Chrift, ftand in as much need of it, as thofe that partake of other Ordinances.

A fixth part of the Worfhip is Ecclefiaftical cenfures, thefe were appointed in the time of the Old Teftament, and are to continue in ufe unto the end of the World, it doth evidently appear, both from the Writings of the *Jews* and likewife from the Scripture, that the *Jews* did make ufe of Ecclefiaftical cenfures, *John* 4. 34, 35. *John* 3. 22. and 12. 42. And it is evident, that thefe cenfures were according

ing

ing to Divine Inſtitution, from *Matth.* 18. 17, 18. Chriſt doth not here make a new Inſtitution for the Goſpel Church, for that Church was not yet in Being, but he urges them to the practiſe of an Old Inſtitution ; if it be enquired where we find any ſuch Inſtitution in the Old Teſtament, I Anſwer, in that expreſſion which we often find in the Old Teſtament, that they ſhould be cut off from *Iſrael*, *Gen.* 17. 14. *Exod.* 12. 14. When one Brother is required to reprove another, and in caſe of Incorrigibleneſs to complain to the Church, that command doth not only bind the Brethren of the ſame Congregation, but alſo the Brethren of any other Congregation ; for there lies the ſame Bond upon us according to opportunity, not to ſuffer ſin in others, as well as in the Members of the ſame Congregation.

There is no need of a particular Inſtitution, who ſhall have the Power of Judgment, to determine whether a Perſon be to be cenſured or not ; it is a part of Rule, and where God appoints Rulers in his Church, he appoints that they ſhall Judge theſe matters; therefore when Chriſt appoints a Paſtor to be a Ruler in the Church, he expreſſes it by having Power of binding and looſing, *Matth.* 16. 19.

A Perſon that is under Church cenſures, is not thereby cut off from his Memberſhip, he ſtands in a Brotherly relation to other Members of the Church, 2 *Theſſ.* 3. 15. Lying under offence and under cenſure for his offence, doth not deprive him of his Viſible Saintſhip, therefore his Children are to be Baptized.

Such offences as are of a more Heinous Nature, don't call for Church cenſures, provided there be a ſuteable Spirit of Repentance ; if the end of cenſures be obtained, there is no occaſion for them ; Perſons under the ſentence of Excommunication, are not only to be debarred from the Lords Supper, but alſo to be exclued from the familiar Society of the People of God ; where there is no ſpecial Bond, we are not to have that Society with them, that we may have with Heathens, 1 *Cor.* 5. 9, 12.

To this Act of Worſhip appertains Abſolution, when the Perſon that hath offended doth manifeſt a Spirit of Repentance, whether he has been cenſured or not, he is to be acquited.

The ſeventh Act of Worſhip is the Bleſſing of the Congregation ; there is a Bleſſing of Men by way of ſupplication, that may be performed by any Perſon, and there is a Bleſſing by way of Confirmation, this is pronounced in the Name of God ; this is either extraordinary, by way of prediction, ſo the Patriarchs did bleſs

G   their

their Children, and others endued with a Prophetical Spirit, did bless the People, as *Moses* ; or else ordinary, pronounced in Gods Name by ordinary Ministers ; this may either be pronounced by way of assertion, as when the Minister doth say, *Blessed are they that bear the Word of God and do it* ; Or in way of supplication, as when he saith, *The Grace of the Lord Jesus Christ be with you* ; Yet this is more then a Prayer, *Viz.* A Declaration in Gods Name what shall come to pass, and therefore it must be understood in such a way as is according to Gods Covenant, *Deut.* 20. 34. *God appointed the Priests of Old to Bless the People*, Numb. 6. 23. And this work seems to be a common work to the rest of the Levites, who were teachers in *Israel, Deut.* 10. 8. There is no need of any new Institution in the Gospel, impowring Ministers to bless in the Name of God, it being a proper part of the work of a Minister ; Christ by appointing Ministers, hath appointed Men to bless the People ; yet that seems to be Instituted, *Matth.* 10. 12, 13. *Deut.* 21. 5.

Such Men as are Preachers of the Gospel, yet not separated to that work by Ordination, have no Power to bless the Congregation, because this depends meerly upon Institution, therefore is not to be done, but according to Institution.

Ministers being appointed to bless Authoritatively in the Name of God, it is utterly improper for them to speak in the first Person, including themselves, *Numb.* 6. 24. It is also improper for them to Bless the Church of God, that are dispersed all over the World.

C H A P.

CHAP. VIII.

Of Churches confisting of Divers Congregations.

A Church confisting of Divers Congregations, is a Society of Divers Congregational Churches, joyning together according to Gods appointment, for the constant carrying on of the Publick Worship of God; such Churches are acknowledged in the greatest Part of Protestant Churches; but some in latter times do make a Question whether there be any such Churches.

That there are National Churches, does appear, *First*, from the light of Nature, the light of Nature teaches us, that Man was made for the Worship of God, that Man is fitted for Society, and the great end why he is so, is, that in Society he may carry on the Worship of God, and as the light of Nature teaches us, that lesser Societies ought to carry on the Worship of God in Conjunction, so that Kingdoms and Countrys should joyn together in promoting and advancing the Worship of God; it is most agreeable to the light of Nature, that they that are one People, should Unite together in carrying on Gods Worship, and should have Power to regulate and govern the several parts of that Body. Nature teaches, that every Kingdom should see that the Worship and Ordinances of God, be attended in the several Congregations therein.

2dly, From Gods appointing the Nation of the *Jews* to be one Church, *Act.* 7. 38. And God has not appointed any new forms of Churches in the times of the New Testament; there are no other kinds of Churches appointed now; Congregational Churches are no new kind of Churches, but according to the Old Institution; for every Synagogue of the *Jews* was a Congregational Church, they had Ecclesiastical Rule and Government in them; they are called Churches by Christ, *Matth.* 18. 17. That the Old Testament Institution doth continue still, appears partly because the Christian Churches of the *Jews* were subordinate to the National Church of the *Jews*; they were Members of the National Church, and did attend *Jewish* Ordinances; and therefore by Institution, Christian
Congre-

Congregations are not abſolute, but Subordinate to a National Church ; it is further evident, becauſe the *Jewiſh* National Church did not ceaſe as their Ceremonies did, becauſe their Date was out, but becauſe they rejected Chriſt, *Rom.* 11. 20. Had they kept Gods Covenant, they would have continued a National Church to this Day.

3*ly,* From the Publick Covenant that is between God and a profeſſing People ; God made a Publick Covenant between him and the People of *Iſrael,* wherein he engages publick Proſperity unto them, upon condition of their obedience ; and all profeſſing Countries are under the ſame Covenant for ſubſtance; the promiſes, and ſo the threatnings declared are of force unto the end of the World, and we have the like encouragement to obedience that they had, and are in the like danger in caſe of diſobedience.

God deals with profeſſing Countrys at this Day according to the Tenor of that Covenant, thoſe promiſes will never be out of Date to the end of the World, God makes the ſame to *Iſrael* with reſpect to the time of their Reſtoration, this abundantly Witneſſeth that every Chriſtian Nation is a Church ; if God hath made a Covenant with them upon condition of obedience, then they are a Society in Covenant with God, then they are one body in Covenant with God, and the whole hath Power over the parts, and they are inveſted with ſufficient Authority to ſee the Covenant kept : If they were in Covenant, and had not Power to make the ſeveral parts to keep Covenant, the Covenant would be a ſnare to them ; particular Societies might bring guilt upon them, and they would have no Power to remove it ; if they be all engaged in one individual Covenant, the Country hath Power to regulate all Maleadminiſtrations that any of the parts are guilty of, if they are in one individual Covenant, they are as one body Expoſed by God, the People of God, the flock of Chriſt, and therefore one Church ; here is all that made *Iſrael* to be a Church, therefore ſuch a People are a Church.

4*ly,* From the promiſes that God hath made of making Gentile Nations to be his People ; God did not only promiſe to ſet up ſome Churches among the Gentiles, but to take whole Nations into Covenant with himſelf, *Iſa.* 24. 22. And it is expreſly foretold by Chriſt that whole Nations ſhould receive the Goſpel, and become Churches, *Matth.* 21. 43. Yea, the Scripture declareth that when *Iſrael* is Converted, they ſhall be in the ſame Covenant as formerly, the ſame promiſes are made to them in *Ezekiel,* as the Fruits of their obedience, as were made to them in *Deutronomy* ; and if the whole *Jewiſh*
Nation

Nation will be one Church, when they are restored, then it will be so with every other Christian Nation, the difference between *Jews* and *Gentiles* is now abolished.

5. Because the supream Ecclesiastical Authority doth not lye in particular Congregations; if there be no National Church, then every particular Congregation is absolute and independant, and not responsable to any higher Power: This is too Lordly a principle, it is too ambitious a thing for every small Congregation to arrogate such an uncontroulable Power, and to be accountable to none on Earth; this is neither a probable way for the Peace of Churches, nor for the safety of Church Members; appeals are admitted in all Kingdoms; and it is more probable that in a whole Country, Persons may be found that may rectify the Miscarriages of particular Congregations, then that particular Congregations will not miscarry; this absoluteness of particular Congregations is a dignity that the primitive Churches did not enjoy, this is not the common Priviledge of Gospel Churches; the primitive Churches were under the Government of the Apostles, and it seems that God gave them this Power, because the ordinary way of Government could not then be practised, the greater part of all Gentile Nations lying in their Heathenism.

Obj. 1. *We don't find in the New Testament, any National Church among the Gentiles.*

Answ. The reason of that is, not that National Churches are not according to the mind of God, in the Days of the New Testament, but because there was no Nation that did receive the Christian faith. Tho there were many Congregations gathered among the Gentiles, yet there were very few of them, comparitively, that did entertain the Gospel; the bulk of all the Gentile Nations, lay in their Heathenism, during all that time that we have the History of in the Scriptures.

Obj. 2. *God hath not appointed in the New Testament any National Officers, as the High Priest in* Israel, *nor any National place of Worship as* Jerusalem, *therefore there is no National Church.*

Answ. 1. To have one National Officer over the whole, is not essential to the being of a National Church; *Israel* was a National Church, when they had no such National Officers, while the first Born did Exercise the Office of the Priests, before the separation of the Levites to that work. There be several sorts of civil Government, none of which are essential to a Republick. The being of a National Church doth not necessitate this or that form of Government

H   ment,

ment : If there be a National Church, it follows that there muſt be ſome to Rule over the whole, but that this Power ſhould reſide either ſolely, or principally in one Man, doth not follow at all. It was ſuteable to the State of the *Jewiſh* Church, that there ſhould be one ſupream Officer to be a Type of Chriſt ; but now there being no ſuch occaſion, the Church may be governed without any ſuch.

2. To have one National place of Worſhip, is but accidental to a National Church ; *Iſrael* was a National Church in *Egypt*, yet had no National place of Worſhip ; all the Worſhip of God, beſides that which was tipical, might be attended in their Synagogues. The not having a National place of Worſhip, is no hinderance to their being Governed by a National Authority. There may be a National Government as well without, as with a National place of Worſhip.

This National Church is to be divided into provincial, and thoſe again ſubdivided into Claſſical. The Light of Nature teaches us to make ſuch Diviſions of great Political Bodies, that Government may be more eaſily managed. Natural prudence teaches Men in the civil State, to make ſuch Subordination of Courts of Juſtice, for the benefit of the Common Wealth. This is according to the Counſel which was given to *Moſes*, by his father in Law, and approved by God, *Exod.* 18. By the ſame Rule that the whole is to Rule over the parts, the greater parts are to Rule over the leſſer parts, for a greater part, is an whole reſpecting the leſſer parts into which it is divided. A County is a part with reſpect to a Province, but an whole with reſpect to the ſeveral Congregations therein, and accordingly may Exerciſe Government over them ; yet with Subordination to that Authority that is over the whole. A gradation both in Civil and Eccleſiaſtical Authority is founded in the very Law of Nature.

Obj. *If we grant a National Church under the Goſpel, we may as well grant an Oecumenical Church : thoſe that plead for the Juriſdiction of Synods, refer things at laſt to the Judgment of an Oecumenical Synod.*

Anſw. There is no ſuch thing as an inſtitutedOecumenical Church; there is a Catholick Church, but that Notes all thoſe that profeſs the true Religion ; but there is no Inſtituted Oecumenical Church, for the ſeveral Chriſtian Nations are not in the ſame Covenant ; they are indeed in the ſame ſpecial Covenant, but not in the ſame individual Covenant ; ſo it is here, one Nation may keep Covenant, while other Nations braek Covenant.

Neither

Neither is there any Inſtitution for Oecumenical Synods ; if they could convene, they have no Authority ; their conſultations might be of ſome uſe to others, but they have no Authority. A National Synod, is the higheſt Eccleſiaſtical Authority upon Earth.

CHAP. IX.

Of the Government of National Churches.

SUch Proteſtants as have acknowledged National Churches, have been divided about the form of Government to be practiſed among them ; ſome of them are for a mixt Government, partly by Arch-Biſhops, and Biſhops, and partly by Synods, ſo the Church of *England* ; Some have Governed by a Synod alone, ſo the Church of *Scotland* ; and this Government ſeems moſt Conſonant to the Word of God. Synods have been generally acknowledged in all Churches, but upon differing grounds, ſome have founded them upon that Rule of prudence, *Prov.* 24. 66. *In the Multitude of Counſellers there is ſafety,* but if they be grounded upon this, they have no other work but to counſel and adviſe, and they can have no Authority ; all Eccleſiaſtical Authority does depend upon an Inſtitution, their Authority muſt be derived from God. Some do found it upon that Example, *Act.* 15. But this was not properly a Synod, this was not the meeting of the Elders of many Churches, but of the Apoſtles and Elders of the Church of *Jeruſalem*, together with the Brethren ; yet no doubt but the Apoſtles, who were part of that Aſſembly, had the Power of a Synod. But the Foundation of Synods is partly that Publick Covenant, which is between God and his People, partly his Inſtitution in the Old Teſtament, and partly the Rules laid down for the Churches to walk by in the New Teſtament.

1. This Publick Covenant ſhews that the whole muſt Rule the parts. The Rule and Government doth fundamentally belong unto the Church ; the Church hath a right to Govern it ſelf. Thus it is Originally with all Nations as to their civil Government, ſo alſo as to Eccleſiaſtical, and therefore the Exerciſe of this Government muſt be in the hands of ſome that do legally repreſent the whole ; if it be not by ſome that repreſent the whole, then the whole do
not

not Govern, the Rulers muſt be the repreſentation of the whole Church. Thus it is with a Synod, they are either the Elders of the ſeveral Churches, if the Country be not too Numerous, or ſuch as are choſen by the Elders, if the Country be large and numerous, and theſe are a legal repreſentation of the Churches; the Elders of the Churches are choſen to that Office, to be Rulers of the ſeveral Churches, and in caſe there be need. They have Power to ſelect out of themſelves, ſuch a Company as may conveniently meet, with whom their Power ſhall be entruſted. The Light of Nature teaches, that the Government muſt be committed to ſuch a Number, as ſhall not be uncapable by reaſon of their Number, to aſſemble and diſcourſe together, for otherwiſe the Government of the Church would not be a thing practicable.

Thus it is not with Biſhops, they do not legally repreſent the Church; for they are not choſen by the Church, they are not Perſons elected by the Church to Act in their behalf, but are put into their Office by civil Authority; and how can they repreſent the Church who do not deſire any Authority from the Church; and ſecondly, their Office is not of Divine Inſtitution, and how can they who are not of Divine appointment, legally repreſent the Church? Thoſe whoſe Office is not acknowledged in the Law of God, cannot legally repreſent the Church of God.

2. The Church of the *Jews* was Governed by a Counſel of ſeventy two Perſons. Some are of Opinion that the *Jews* had both an Eccleſiaſtical and a civil *Sanedrim*, this is evident, that in Chriſts time they had a Councel that did conſiſt in a great part of the Prieſts, *Act.* 14. 6. and 22. 30. And that God appointed the Prieſts and other Judges to joyn together in hearing of Controverſies, *Deut.* 19. 17. So alſo that there was an aſſembly of the chief of the Prieſts and Levites, appointed by *Jehoſhaphat* to hear Eccleſiaſtical cauſes, 2 *Chron.* 19. 8. And that the High Prieſt was over them in thoſe Eccleſiaſtical cauſes, *v.* 11. By theſe things it is evident, that the Church of *Iſrael* was Governed by an Aſſembly of the Principal Men of the Church. Chriſt Jeſus doth approve of their form of Government that was in his time, *Matth.* 23. 2, 3. By Prieſts, Scribes, Phariſees. By this it is not only evident, that the Government of a National or Provincial Church, by an Aſſembly of its Principal Elders, is a proper ſuteable and hopeful way; but likewiſe that this way is to be obſerved in Chriſtian Nations, ſeeing no other Proviſion is made for their Government; many of the appointments that God made for the *Jewiſh* Church, do continue in force ſtill, and this among the reſt, no other Proviſion being made

yet

yet it does not follow that our Assemblies must have any standing president, as the *Jewish* Assemblies had their High Priest, who was their president, and was a Type of *Christ*; neither does it follow, that we are limitted to the same Number that they were, Circumstances being a sufficient reason for a variation in such cases.

3. The appointment of *Christ*, that Teaching and Ruling Elders should Govern the Church, shews the Power of Synods; these are appointed by Christ to be the Rulers of the Church, 1 *Tim.* 5. 17. *Heb.* 13. 17. There are no other appointed to be Rulers of the Church since the Age of the Apostles, therefore the Government of the National Church must be in their hands; none but they have any Interest in the Publick Government; there is no Warrant from the Word of God to intrust the Government in the hands of any others, and there is sufficient Warrant for them, to take upon them the Government of the National Church, and this by Virtue of their Office. If there be a Publick Covenant, every Church is bound in Conjunction with others to see the Covenant kept, and their Rulers, with whom their Power is intrusted, are bound by Virtue of their Office, to joyn with others to see their Covenant kept; so that their Acting in a synod, is not by Virtue of any New Office. A Minister by Virtue of his Ministerial function, hath Power in Conjunction with others, to Govern the National or Provincial Church.

Obj. If Ministers have a Bond upon them, to joyn with others in the Rule of the National or Provincial Church, then they seem in their own Persons to be bound to attend that Service; which if all should do in National Synods, the Synods would be so large a Body, that they could not Discourse together, and it would be an intollerable prejudice to their Congregations, being much deprived of their Labours.

Answ. The Power of Intrusting delegates is Warranted by the Light and Law of Nature, there being a necessity of it for the good Government of Societies, and there is no necessity of a particular Institution in this case; the necessity of humane affairs does require that Government be intrusted with such a Number that it may be managed to advantage to the Publick, neither is there any hazard of being involved in guilt by such a method; a select Number of the most Prudent and Holy of the Elders, are as likely to Govern the

I

Church

Church according to the mind of God, as the whole Body of the Elders of a Nation.

CHAP. X.

Of the Power of Synods.

THE Power of Synods doth consist principally in these things.

1. They are to teach the People, they are to hold forth Light unto the Church, that was a part of the work of the *Sanedrim* at *Jerusalem*, to teach the People the will of God, *Matth.* 23. 2, 3. That was the special work of the Levites, *Deut.* 38. 10. That Assembly mentioned, *Act.* 15. Met together to give Light to the People of God.

It is very meet that Synods do Publish confessions of faith, not only to bear Testimony to the World, and other *Christian* Kingdoms, of their acknowledging the Truth, but especially to be a Light unto the Churches, to guide them in the way of Life, this hath generally been practised by the Synods of the reformed Churches.

They should particularly Vindicate the Truth, and bear their Testimony against those Errors that are Springing up, *Act.* 15. 24. It is meet also in case of Corruptions in manners, that they do declare what the mind of God is, and Vindicate the Rule; that, if it be possible, they may root out such Licentious principles as are prevailing amongst the People, and advise them to repent of such degeneracies as bring down the Judgments of God. Yet no Man is bound to receive the Doctrines, or practise the Rules held forth by a Synod, because they are taught by them. A Synod is not infallible, and
therefore

therefore no Rule, or Doctrine, is to be taken up on trust from them ; Men do owe that respect to a Synod, as 'tis an Ordinance of God, solemnly to weigh the Doctrines held forth thereby, but they are not to receive them by an implicite faith ; we are bound to prove all things, and if a Man do practise against the Light of his own Conscience, because a Synod hath otherwise determined, he greatly sins, *Rom.* 14. 23. The Synod may direct him in a wrong way, and no Man can be bound to any thing that God has forbidden, *Deut.* 13. 3.

2. They are to bind and loose, to inflict Ecclesiastical censures, or to take them off ; the supream Ecclesiastical Authority must have Power of Judgment, that so there may no publick guilt lye upon the Church ; if they have not Power of Judgment, Particular Persons may be oppressed by the rigour of Presbyteries, and many irregularities committed by the Church, whereby the Country doth become guilty, and there would be no sufficient way to deliver the Land from guilt. Synods have Power to Admonish, to Excommunicate, and deliver from those censures, and every Man must stand to the Judgment of the National Synod, *Deut.* 17. 12.

They are to Judge in case of Complaint ; when any Person Judges himself wronged by the Judgment of a particular Church, and complains to a Synod, they are to hear the case, and upon the hearing of it, not to advise the Church either to confirm the sentence, or to take it off ; but if there be occasion, they are to take off the sentence and restore the Man unto his priviledge.

They are to judge in case of other Complaints ; if any Man hath a Complaint against another, and cannot obtain a hearing in the Church that he belongs unto, or if the Elders of a particular Church be Complained of for any Male-Administration, or if a Church with the Elders be complained of for Heresie, or other scandalous Corruption, the Synod is to hear and Judge the case, and they may not only censure particular Persons, but whole Churches also in case of need.

3. Synods

3. Synods have Power to overfee the calling of Perfons to the Miniftry, and to appoint thofe who fhall examine them ; if the Synod have the Government of the Church in their hands, tho they fhould not abridge Congregations of their Liberty, yet they fhould fee that Churches Act regularly, and that none fhould be fet in the Miniftry but fuch as are duely qualified, therefore it belongs them to appoint meet Perfons to examine fuch as are called to the Miniftry, and to teftify their approbation by the laying on of hands, *Tit.* 1. 5.

The appointing of Ceremonies of Worfhip is properly the work of Jefus Chrift ; the making of orders concerning the external concernments of the Church, is properly the work of the Civil Magiftrate ; but the appointment of fuch as fhall overfee the calling of Perfons to the Miniftry, doth properly belong to the Ecclefiaftical Authority.

FINIS.

RESEARCH LIBRARY

OF

COLONIAL AMERICANA

An Arno Press Collection

Histories

Acrelius, Israel. **A History of New Sweden; Or, The Settlements on the River Delaware** . . . Translated with an Introduction and Notes by William M. Reynolds. Historical Society of Pennsylvania, MEMOIRS, XI, Philadelphia, 1874.

Belknap, Jeremy. **The History of New Hampshire.** 3 vols., Vol. 1—Philadelphia, 1784 (Reprinted Boston, 1792), Vol. 2—Boston, 1791, Vol. 3—Boston, 1792.

Browne, Patrick. **The Civil and Natural History of Jamaica.** In Three Parts . . . London, 1756. Includes 1789 edition Linnaean index.

[Burke, Edmund]. **An Account of the European Settlements in America.** In Six Parts . . . London, 1777. Two volumes in one.

Chalmers, George. **An Introduction to the History of the Revolt of the American Colonies:** Being a Comprehensive View of Its Origin, Derived From the State Papers Contained in the Public Offices of Great Britain. London, 1845. Two volumes in one.

Douglass, William. **A Summary, Historical and Political, of the First Planting, Progressive Improvements, and Present State of the British Settlements in North-America.** Boston, 1749–1752. Two volumes in one.

Edwards, Bryan. **The History, Civil and Commercial, of the British Colonies in the West Indies.** Dublin, 1793–1794. Two volumes in one.

Hughes, Griffith. **The Natural History of Barbados.** In Ten Books. London, 1750.

[Franklin, Benjamin]. **An Historical Review of the Constitution and Government of Pennsylvania, From Its Origin** . . . London, 1759.

Hubbard, William. **A General History of New England, From the Discovery to MDCLXXX.** (*In* Massachusetts Historical Society, COLLECTIONS, Series 2, vol. 5, 6, 1815. Reprinted 1848.)

Hutchinson, Thomas. **The History of the Colony of Massachusetts Bay** . . . 3 vols., Boston, 1764–1828.

Keith, Sir William. **The History of the British Plantations in America** . . . London, 1738.

Long, Edward. **The History of Jamaica:** Or, General Survey of the Antient and Modern State of that Island . . . 3 vols., London, 1774.

Mather, Cotton. **Magnalia Christi Americana;** Or, The Ecclesiastical History of New-England From . . . the Year 1620, Unto the Year . . . 1698. In Seven Books. London, 1702.

Mather, Increase. **A Relation of the Troubles Which Have Hapned in New-England, By Reason of the Indians There From the Year 1614 to the Year 1675** . . . Boston, 1677.

Smith, Samuel. **The History of the Colony of Nova-Caesaria, Or New-Jersey** . . . **to the Year 1721** . . . Burlington, N.J., 1765.

Thomas, Sir Dalby. **An Historical Account of the Rise and Growth of the West-India Collonies,** and of the Great Advantages They are to England, in Respect to Trade. London, 1690.

Trumbull, Benjamin. **A Complete History of Connecticut,** Civil and Ecclesiastical, From the Emigration of Its First Planters, From England, in the Year 1630, to the Year 1764; and to the Close of the Indian Wars . . . New Haven, 1818. Two volumes in one.

Personal Narratives and Promotional Literature

Byrd, William. **The Secret Diary of William Byrd of Westover, 1709–1712,** edited by Louis B. Wright and Marion Tinling. Richmond, Va., 1941.

Byrd, William. **The London Diary (1717–1721) and Other Writings,** edited by Louis B. Wright and Marion Tinling. New York, 1958.

A Genuine Narrative of the Intended Conspiracy of the Negroes at Antigua. Extracted From an Authentic Copy of a Report, Made to the Chief Governor of the Carabee Islands, by the Commissioners, or Judges Appointed to Try the Conspirators. Dublin, 1737.

Gookin, Daniel. **An Historical Account of the Doings and Sufferings of the Christian Indians in New England in the Years 1675, 1676, 1677** . . . (*In* American Antiquarian Society, Worcester, Mass. ARCHAEOLOGIA AMERICANA. TRANSACTIONS AND COLLECTIONS. Cambridge, 1836. vol. 2.)

Gookin, Daniel. **Historical Collections of the Indians in New England.** Of Their Several Nations, Numbers, Customs, Manners, Religion and Government, Before the English Planted There . . . Boston, 1792.

Morton, Thomas. **New English Canaan or New Canaan.** Containing an Abstract of New England, Composed in Three Books . . . Amsterdam, 1637.

Sewall, Samuel. **Diary of Samuel Sewall, 1674–1729.** (*In* Massachusetts Historical Society. COLLECTIONS, 5th Series, V–VII, 1878–1882.) Three volumes.

Virginia: Four Personal Narratives. (Hamor, Ralph. *A True Discourse on the Present Estate of Virginia . . . Till the 18 of June 1614 . . .* London, 1615/Hariot, Thomas. *A Briefe and True Report of the New Found Land of Virginia . . .* London, 1588/Percy, George. *A Trewe Relacyon of the Proceedings and Ocurrentes of Momente Which Have Happened in Virginia From . . . 1609, Until . . . 1612.* (In *Tyler's Quarterly Historical and Genealogical Magazine,* Vol. III, 1922.) /Rolf, John. *Virginia in 1616.* (In *Virginia Historical Register and Literary Advertiser,* Vol. I, No. III, July, 1848.) New York, 1972.

Winthrop, John. **The History of New England From 1630–1649.** Edited by James Savage. Boston, 1825–1826. Two volumes in one.

New England Puritan Tracts of the Seventeenth Century

Cobbett, Thomas. **The Civil Magistrate's Power in Matters of Religion Modestly Debated** . . . London, 1653.

Cotton, John. **The Bloudy Tenent, Washed, and Made White in the Bloud of the Lambe** . . . London, 1647.

Cotton, John. **A Brief Exposition with Practical Observations Upon the Whole Book of Canticles.** London, 1655.

Cotton, John. **Christ the Fountaine of Life:** Or, Sundry Choyce Sermons on Part of the Fift Chapter of the First Epistle of St. John. London, 1651.

Cotton, John. **Two Sermons.** (*Gods Mercie Mixed with His Justice* . . . London, 1641/*The True Constitution of a Particular Visible Church, Proved by Scripture* . . . London, 1642.) New York, 1972.

Eliot, John. **The Christian Commonwealth:** Or, The Civil Policy of the Rising Kingdom of Jesus Christ. London, 1659.

Hooker, Thomas. **The Application of Redemption,** By the Effectual Work of the Word, and Spirit of Christ, for the Bringing Home of Lost Sinners to God. London, 1657.

H[ooker], T[homas]. **The Christian's Two Chiefe Lessons,** Viz. Selfe Deniall, and Selfe Tryall . . . London, 1640.

Hooker, Thomas. **A Survey of the Summe of Church-Discipline** Wherein the Way of the Churches of New England is Warranted Out of the Word, and All Exceptions of Weight, Which Are Made Against It, Answered . . . London, 1648.

Increase Mather Vs. Solomon Stoddard: Two Puritan Tracts. (Mather, Increase. *The Order of the Gospel, Professed and Practised by the Churches of Christ in New-England* . . . Boston, 1700/Stoddard, Solomon. *The Doctrine of Instituted Churches Explained, and Proved From the Word of God.* London, 1700.) New York, 1972.

Mather, Cotton. **Ratio Disciplinae Fratrum Nov-Anglorum.** A Faithful Account of the Discipline Professed and Practised, in the Churches of New England. Boston, 1726.

Mather, Richard. **Church Covenant:** Two Tracts. (*Church-Government and Church-Covenant Discussed, in an Answer to the Elders of the Severall Churches in New-England* . . . London, 1643/*An Apologie of the Churches in New-England for Church-Covenant, Or, A Discourse Touching the Covenant Between God and Men, and Especially Concerning Church-Covenant* . . . London, 1643.) New York, 1972.

The Imperial System

[Blenman, Jonathan]. **Remarks on Several Acts of Parliament Relating More Especially to the Colonies Abroad** . . . London, 1742.

British Imperialism: Three Documents. (Berkeley, George. *A Proposal for the Better Supplying of Churches in our Foreign Plantations, and for Converting the Savage Americans to Christianity by a College to be Erected in the Summer Islands, Otherwise Called the Isles of Bermuda . . .* London, 1724/[Fothergill, John]. *Considerations Relative to the North American Colonies.* London, 1765/*A Letter to a Member of Parliament Concerning the Naval-Store Bill . . .* London, 1720.) New York, 1972.

Coke, Roger. **A Discourse of Trade** . . . London, 1670.

[D'Avenant, Charles]. **An Essay Upon the Government of the English Plantations on the Continent of America** (1701). An Anonymous Virginian's Proposals for Liberty Under the British Crown, With Two Memoranda by William Byrd. Edited by Louis B. Wright. San Marino, Calif., 1945.

Dummer, Jeremiah. **A Defence of the New-England Charters** . . . London, 1721.

Gee, Joshua. **The Trade and Navigation of Great Britain Considered:** Shewing that Surest Way for a Nation to Increase in Riches, is to Prevent the Importation of Such Foreign Commodities as May Be Rais'd at Home. London, 1729.

[Little, Otis]. **The State of Trade in the Northern Colonies Considered;** With an Account of Their Produce, and a Particular Description of Nova Scotia . . . London, 1748.

Tucker, Jos[iah]. **The True Interest of Britain, Set Forth in Regard to the Colonies:** And the Only Means of Living in Peace and Harmony With Them, Including Five Different Plans for Effecting this Desirable Event . . . Philadelphia, 1776.